Black Settlers in Britain 1555–1958

Nigel File and Chris Power

Heinemann

To past pupils, colleagues, families and friends associated with the former Tulse Hill School, South London

Heinemann Educational
a division of Heinemann Publishers (Oxford) Ltd
Halley Court, Jordan Hill, Oxford OX2 8EJ
OXFORD LONDON EDINBURGH MADRID
ATHENS BOLOGNA PARIS MELBOURNE
SYDNEY AUCKLAND SINGAPORE TOKYO
IBADAN NAIROBI GABORONE HARARE
PORTSMOUTH NH (USA)

©Nigel File and Chris Power 1981
First published 1981
Reprinted 1981, 1984, 1986, 1988

This edition published 1995

95 96 97 98 10 9 8 7 6 5 4 3 2 1

British Library Cataloguing in Publication Data

File, Nigel
    Black Settlers in Britain, 1555–1958.
    1. Blacks—Great Britain—Social life and customs
I. Title   II. Power, Chris
941′.004′96   DA125.N4

ISBN 0 435 310 82 8

ACKNOWLEDGEMENTS

The authors and publishers wish to acknowledge the following either as sources of illustrations of for permission to reproduce them:
Beaney Institute, Canterbury: Fig. 12.2.
British Library Newspaper Library: Figs. 36.1, 40.1, 40.2, 42.4, 42.5, 42.6, 43.1, 43.2, 43.3, 47.1, 47.2, 47.3, 47.4, 48.2, 48.3, 52.1.
British Library (Reference Division): Figs. 1.1, 3.1, 8.1, 10.1, 10.2, 10.3, 10.4, 10.5, 10.6, 11.1, 12.1, 13.2, 13.3, 14.1, 14.2, 15.1, 16.1, 18.1, 19.1, 19.2, 24.1, 25.1, 25.2, 26.1, 27.1, 32.2, 32.3, 32.4, 32.5, 44.1, 44.2, 45.1, 46.1, 46.2, 46.4.
British Library of Political and Economic Science: Fig. 41.2.
British Museum, Department of Prints and Drawings: Figs. 17.1, 30.1, 30.2, 32.1, 33.4, 33.5, 33.6, 34.1.
Drum Arts Workshop: Fig. 37.1.
Gloucestershire Record Office, the Granville Sharp Papers in the Lloyd-Baker Collection (by courtesy of the executors): Fig. 11.2.
G.L.C. Maps and Prints: Figs. 30.3, 33.1.
G.L.C. Photographic Collection: Fig. 46.3.
Robert Harding: Cover.
Donald Hinds: Cover, Figs. 53.1, 53.2, 53.3.
The Controller, H.M.S.O.: Figs. 47.5, 47.6.
Imperial War Museum: Figs. 42.1, 42.2, 42.3.
Imperial War Museum, Department of Printed Books: Figs. 47.5, 47.6.
Dr Johnson's House Trust: Cover.
Mansell Collection: Figs. 9.1, 9.2, 35.1, 38.1.
Minet Library, Lambeth, Surrey Collection: Figs. 15.2, 28.1.
National Maritime Museum, Sailor's Home and Red Ensign Club Collection: Figs. 41.1, 41.3.
Private collection: Fig. 7.2.
Public Record Office: Figs. 20.1, 20.2, 20.3, 20.4, 20.5, 20.6, 21.1, 21.2, 24.2, 24.3, 24.4 (all PRO Treasury Board paper (T1)), 28.2, 29.1, 29.2 (Home Office papers Convicts Miscellaneous (HO 7)).
The Marquess of Salisbury, the Cecil Papers: Fig. 6.1.
Syndication International: Figs. 52.1, 52.2.
The Times: Figs. 47.1, 47.2, 47.3, 47.4, 48.2, 48.3.
Walker Art Gallery, Liverpool: Fig. 7.1.
Acknowledgement is also made to the following:
Chris Abuk for the drawing in Fig. 7.1.
Paul Mukasa for the photographs in Figs. 2.1, 4.1, 13.1, 30.3, 33.2, 39.1, 51.1.
Sibohan Stewart for the photograph in Fig. 33.3.

Contents

Preface

This book shows that Black people have lived in Britain from at least 1555 to the present. It enables readers to trace the part played by Black people in the development of Britain. It depicts individuals who were famous at the time they lived including Olaudah Equiano, Ira Aldridge, Mary Seacole, Samuel Coleridge-Taylor and Lord Constantine. It provides images of ordinary Black people who lived in Britain. Until the 1780s some had to live as slaves and some escaped from slavery. Britain has been drawn into many wars since 1555 and this book depicts Black people's participation in these events, including the American War of Independence, the Napoleonic, the Crimean, the First World and Second World Wars. When we study themes in British history we should always be aware that there has been a diversity of groups in Britain. Pupils and others studying history can be introduced to real historical people represented in this book through portraits and documents.

The book explains how Black people have been treated in Britain. Positively, it reflects how some people fought for freedom, equality and fairness; that in time of war leaders in Britain were thankful that Black people took part. It shows how there were several attempts to expel Black people from Britain and that individuals and groups have suffered insults and violence in each century. This aspect of British history is also something which everyone can know about.

Why Black Settlers? When the first edition of this book was being prepared Europeans in Africa, particularly in what was Rhodesia, were referred to in the media as White Settlers. In Europe Black people were often referred to as guest workers and, in Britain, as immigrants. We chose to call this book *Black Settlers in Britain* to apply a common usage and to challenge the notion that Black people's residence in Britain was a temporary thing. As one South London student wrote. 'Black people have been in Britain a long time and they are here to stay!'

This book focuses on Black people whose origins were in Africa, and subsequently the Caribbean and the Americas, and who were born in Britain or who eventually came to live here. Particularly with regard to the Caribbean and the Americas, many people identify themselves as Black in the context of African and South Asian and East Asian heritages, whatever their skin pigmentation or place of birth. Books by Rozina Visram, in particular, complement this volume with coverage of the Asian experience in Britain. In the 1980s and 1990s more people and groups have researched Britain's multi-ethnic, and multi-cultural history and this is reflected in the large resources list. The book was put together with support and encouragement from a wide group of people who shared family stories, discovered additional material, helped us access archives and provided contextual dialogue. It reflects collaborative work in a community since the 1970s and the aspirations that community had for future generations.

The Numbers Game 1

Some people think that black people came to Britain only after 1945. It seems odd that the writer in Fig. 1.1 is complaining of 20,000 Negro servants in London in 1764—too many, apparently, when the total population of London was only 676,250.

How many were there exactly? Nobody knows for sure. Granville Sharp was one man likely to know at that time how many black people there were in London (see page 17). Writing in 1768 he agreed that there were about 20,000.

The total number of people in London then can also only be estimated. We have accepted the estimate of the famous London historian, M. Dorothy George.

Black people were often referred to as negroes and blackamoors at this time. The writer in Fig. 1.1 does this.

This book will show that many black people were free and were not slaves.

1.1 From *The Gentleman's Magazine*, vol. 34, 1764, p. 493.

The practice of importing Negroe servants into these kingdoms is said to be already a grievance that requires a remedy, and yet it is every day encouraged, insomuch that the number in this metropolis only, is supposed to be near 20,000; the main objections to their importation is, that they cease to consider themselves as slaves in this free country, nor will they put up with an inequality of treatment, nor more willingly perform the laborious offices of servitude than our own people, and if put to do it, are generally sullen spiteful, treacherous, and revengeful. It is therefore highly impolitic to introduce them as servants here, where that rigour and severity is impracticable which is absolutely necessary to make them useful.

The mortality among the horned cattle rages in *Saxony* to a terrible degree. Inoculation has been practised in other countries with success, and is recommended to the sufferers there as the most effectual means to prevent the loss of their herds. (*See Vol.* xxix. *p.* 426.)

More information

M. Dorothy George, *London Life in the Eighteenth Century* (Penguin, 1966/Peregrine, 1976).

2 Francis Barber

Francis Barber (Fig. 2.1) was born in Jamaica and was brought to England in 1750 by a Captain Bathurst. Francis was sent to school at Barton in Yorkshire. Capt. Bathurst died in 1752 and gave Francis his freedom.

Francis then became a servant to Dr. Samuel Johnson, a friend of the Bathurst family. Dr. Johnson is most famous as the man who made the first English dictionary. Dr. Johnson sent Francis to school at Bishops Stortford, Hertfordshire. Francis Barber lived with him at his house off Fleet Street, and also at Streatham Place in South London, for many years.

When Dr. Johnson died in 1782 Francis was left his property, an income of £70 a year and all his books and personal possessions. Francis then moved to Lichfield with his wife, Elizabeth, whom he had married in 1776. They ran a school at Burntwood, near Lichfield, until Francis became ill. He died in January 1801 at Stafford Infirmary. Elizabeth Barber carried on teaching for another fifteen years.

Elizabeth and Francis Barber had four children. One of them, Samuel, was a Methodist minister and one grandson emigrated to the United States. Another continued to live in the Staffordshire area.

2.1   Francis Barber.

More information

Aleyn L. Reade, *Johnsonian Gleanings*; Part II, *Francis Barber* (London, 1912).
'Memoir of Samuel Barber, *The Primitive Methodist Magazine*, 10, 1829.

Olaudah Equiano 3

3.1 Olaudah Equiano, from *Equiano's Travels*.

Olaudah Equiano (Fig. 3.1) knew about slavery from his own personal experience. When he was 10 he was taken from the Benin coast to Barbados as a slave, and moved to Virginia before ending up as a servant to a ship's captain.

Between 1757 and 1763 he went with his master, Captain Pascal, on naval service to the Caribbean, the Mediterranean and North America. He stayed for part of that time at Blackheath in London with the Guerin family who taught him to read. In 1759 he was baptised at St. Margaret's Church, Westminster.

Slavery, however, was not a thing of the past for Olaudah. In 1763 Captain Pascal realised that Olaudah was going to assert his right to freedom, so he had him shipped to the Americas where he was resold.

Olaudah managed to purchase his freedom in 1766 and, after returning to England, spent the next eleven years as a merchant seaman. In 1773 he was a member of Phipp's expedition to Greenland.

Olaudah was determined to fight slavery in every way he could. In 1789 he wrote his life story, which was widely used in the anti-slavery campaign. He travelled extensively speaking against slavery—Birmingham, Sheffield, Bristol, Hull, Devizes, Belfast and Dublin were some of the places visited in the 1790s.

Olaudah was employed in 1786 by the Navy Commissioners as commissary in charge of stores for the black settlers who were being sent to Sierra Leone. He soon found out that the preparations were inadequate and the shipping agent was taking supplies intended for the settlers. Olaudah spoke out against this, was dismissed from the job, criticised in the press, and only later vindicated and compensated. Olaudah died in 1801 before abolition and emancipation was achieved. In 1792 he had married Susan Cullen who came from Ely, Cambridgeshire. Their daughter Anna Maria died in 1797 aged four and is buried at Chesterton in north Cambridgeshire (see Fig. 33.3).

Olaudah was also known by the name Gustavus Vasa or Vassa (see Fig. 25.2).

More information

The moving and exciting life of Equiano is available as *Equiano's Travels*, edited by Paul Edwards, in the African Writers Series. (Heinemann Educational Books).

A facsimile edition of the full text, *The Interesting Narrative of the Life of Olaudah Equiano or Gustavus Vassa, the African*, is published by Dawsons of Pall Mall in their Colonial History Series.

3

4 Ignatius Sancho

Ignatius Sancho (Fig. 4.1) was born on a slave ship in the mid Atlantic and spent the first two years of his life as a slave in Grenada. He was then brought to England as a servant, and he settled here until his death forty-nine years later. His family of six children included a son, William, who became a librarian to Sir Joseph Banks. Ignatius' mistress did not believe in educating him because he would not then have been so servile. He wrote that the family 'judged that ignorance was the best security for obedience.'

He was spotted by the Duke of Montagu who had already helped Job ben Solomon and the black Jamaican poet, Francis Williams. He was introduced to the Duchess of Montagu and given books to read. Ignatius' mistress did not like this and even threatened to 'return Ignatius Sancho to his African slavery'. Shortly after the Duke's death in 1749 Sancho fled to seek the Duchess's protection. She finally agreed to employ him as a butler. On her death she left him £70 and an annuity of £30.

Later he married a black West Indian woman and ran a grocer's shop in Charles Street, Westminster. With six children he was not very well off, and in 1779 wrote that he was 'never poorer since created—but 'tis a general case—Blessed times for a poor Blacky grocer to hang or drown in.' Returning from Vauxhall one evening with his family, Sancho recorded, 'We went by water—had a coach home—were gazed at, etc. etc.—but not much abused.' But later, 'they stopped us in town, and most generously insulted us'. The man they insulted had mixed with some of the most famous people of the time. His portrait was painted by Gainsborough and he was a friend of Garrick, the playwright, and Sterne, the writer.

Ignatius wrote poetry, two plays and a work on music. After his death, on 14 December 1780, his letters were published in a book which had enormous sales. Five editions of this book were produced and his writing was used as evidence to support the movement to end slavery.

He was buried at Westminster Broadway.

4.1 Ignatius Sancho.

Equiano, Barber and Sancho were three well-known black people who lived in the eighteenth century. How was it that people of African origin had come to Britain in the first place?

As more and more voyages had been made to West Africa by English seamen in the sixteenth century some Africans had been brought to English ports then.

John Lok returned from Guinea in 1555 carrying with him, as Hakluyt writes, 'certain black slaves whereof some were tall and strong men and could well agree with our meates and drinkes'. In fact these Africans returned to Africa after they had learnt English to act as interpreters for traders.

Earlier trade links across the Mediterranean, especially involving African gold, combined with the Muslim occupation of Spain, had led to people known as Moors settling in Western Europe. It is therefore probable that people from Africa had been in Britain in earlier times.

English involvement in the African slave trade was pioneered by John Hawkins. Hawkins had been sponsored by Queen Elizabeth I, amongst others. John Hawkins made a great deal of money from trading in slaves. He also sold cloth from England, oranges from the Mediterranean, and brought back hides and sugar. He must have thought, however, that he made most of his money from captured Africans as his crest is of an African in chains (Fig. 5.1).

5.1   Sir John Hawkins's crest.

More information

'The Second Voyage of John Lok, 1554–5' in Richard Hakluyt, *The Principal Navigations, Voiages, Traffiques and Discoveries of the English Nation* 12 vols, VI, p. 176, (Glasgow, 1904).

6 Expulsion?

Africans became increasingly common in English towns. It became fashionable to employ African servants, if you had the money to do so. At this time harsh Poor Laws had been introduced to deal with problems of unemployment and vagrancy. Some people objected to African settlement. In 1596 Queen Elizabeth I issued orders that black people must be sent abroad.

In 1601 a Royal Proclamation was issued stating that all 'negroes and blackamoors' should be speedily expelled from England, and licensing Caspar van Senden to deport them. It is clear that the first order was not successful and there is no evidence as to the success of the second.

The actual proclamation is reproduced in Fig. 6.1 and a line-for-line interpretation of the Elizabethan handwriting is given below:

More information

Acts of the Privy Council, xxvi, 1596–7, 16, 20 and 21.
'Licensing Caspar van Sanden to deport Negroes' (1601) in *Tudor Royal Proclamations, 1588–1603*, ed. J. L. Hughes and J. F. Larkin (Yale U. P. 1969), 221.

Whereas the Queen's majesty, tendering the
good and welfare of her own natural subjects, greatly distressed in these
hard times of dearth, is highly discontented to understand the
great number of Negroes and blackamoors which (as she is informed)
5 are crept into this realm since the troubles between her highness
and the King of Spain; who are fostered and relieved here, to
the great annoyance of her own liege people
who want the relief which these people consume, as also for that
the most of them are infidels having no understanding of Christ
10 or his Gospel: hath given especial commandment that the said kind
of people shall be with all speed avoided and discharged out of this
her majesty's dominions; and to that end and purpose hath appointed Casper
van Senden, merchant of Lubeck, for their speedy transportation, a man
that hath very well deserved of this realm in respect that by his own
15 labour and charge he hath relieved and brought from Spain divers
of our English nation, who otherwise would have perished there. These
shall therefore be to will and require you and every[one] of you to aid
and assist the said Casper van Senden, or his associates to take up
such Negroes and blackamoors to be transported as aforesaid, as
20 he shall find within the realm of England; and if there shall
be any person or persons which are possessed of any such blackamoors
that refuse to deliver them in sort as aforesaid, then
we require you to call them before you and to advise and persuade
them by all good means to satisfy her majesty's pleasure therein,
25 which if they shall eftsoons [soon afterwards] willfully and obstinately
refuse, we pray you then to certify their names unto us,
to the end her majesty may take such further course therein as
it shall seem best in her princely wisdom.

6.1 From an Elizabethan
Proclamation.

... prayeng the Queenes maᵗⁱᵉˢ touching the
weale and welfare of her owne naturall subiectes greatly distressed in this
present tyme of dearth, is highly discontented to understande the
great nomber of Negars and Blackamoores, wᶜʰ (as she is enformed)
5 are crepte into this Realme since the troubles betweene her highnes
and the kinge of Spaine, who are fostered and powered here to
the greate annoyance of her owne liege people, that
wante the reliefe, wᶜʰ those people consume, as also for that
the moste of them are infidells, havinge noe understandinge of Christe
10 or his gospell; hath geven especiall comaundemᵗ, that the saide kinde
of people shoulde be wᵗʰ all speede avoyded and discharged out of this
her maᵗⁱᵉˢ Dominions; And to that end and purpose hath appoynted Casper
van Zenden, merchante of Lubeck, for theire speedie transportacion, a man
that hath bene well deserved of this Realme, in respect, that by his owne
15 labor and charge he hath relieved and brought for Spaine and Portingale
of oᵘʳ Englishe nation, who otherwise would have perished there: These
shall therefore be to will and require yᵒᵘ and everie of yᵒᵘ to aide
and assiste the saide Casper van Zenden, or his assignes, to take upp
suche Negars and Blackamoores to be transported, as aforesaide, as
20 he shall finde within the Realme of Englande; And yf there shalbe
anye person or persons, wᶜʰ are possessed of anye suche Blackamoores
that refuse to deliver them in sorte as aforesaide: Then
we require yᵒᵘ to call them before you, and to advise and persuade
them by all good meanes to satisfie her maᵗⁱᵉˢ pleasure therein,
25 wᶜʰ if they shall eftsoones wilfully and obstinatlie
refuse; we praye yᵒᵘ then to certifie theire names unto us,
to thend her maᵗⁱᵉ maye take suche further course therein as
yᵗ shall seeme best in her princelie wisdome.

7 The Trade

People were at the centre of the slave trade. Some benefited. These were the planters and merchants. Few of them lived on their estates overseas. Instead they lived in Britain. Some of the families were: the Beckfords, the Codringtons and the Longs.

The people who suffered were, first of all, the indentured labourers from England, and later the Africans who were captured and turned into slaves. Their children, if they survived, were born in bondage and many died struggling for their freedom.

The slave pictured in the family portrait (Fig. 7.1) of Sir William Young, who owned a plantation in Antigua, probably lived with the family at their house in Delaford, Buckinghamshire. The slave of the 3rd Duke of Perth (Fig. 7.2) wears a collar.

More information

R. S. Dunn, *Sugar and Slaves* (London, Jonathan Cape, 1973).

E. Williams, *Capitalism and Slavery* (London, Andre Deutsch, 1964).

7.1 *The Family of Sir William Young* by J. Zoffany.

7.2 James Drummond, 3rd Duke of Perth with his slave.

People for Sale 8

The advertisement in Fig. 8.1 was not placed in a Jamaican, Barbadian or Virginian newspaper, but in the *Daily Advertiser*, London, on 13 December 1744.

Human beings weren't only sold in places abroad but in England itself.

8.1   From the *Daily Advertiser*, 13 December 1744.

Wanted for the West-Indies directly,

TWO Journeymen Taylors, one that can undertake the Part of a Finisher, and can cut out well; the other to be a good Workman at the making Part.

Any such who are willing to go, may, by enquiring at the Bar of the Rainbow Coffee-House in Ironmonger-Lane, hear of a Place much to their Advantage.

To be SOLD,

A Pretty little Negro Boy, about nine Years old, and well limb'd. If not dispos'd of, is to be sent to the West Indies in six Days Time.

He is to be seen at the Dolphin Tavern in Tower-Street.

To be SOLD,

A Clear Rent-Charge, from 100l. to 200l. a Year, to be secur'd out of a Freehold Estate of a proper Value. Any Person who wants the above may direct for Mr. Leneufe, at the Bar of Somerset Coffee-House opposite to the New Church in the Strand, where they may be waited on Tomorrow or Saturday next.

SCOTCH HOLLANDS, of the best Fabrick and Colour, are sold, cheaper than any where else in Town, at the Mary Queen of Scots's Head, next Shop but one to Cecil-Street in the Strand.

9 Servants/Slaves

Black people were pictured in many prints as servants—see
Figs. 9.1–9.2.

Unfortunately there are no records available to tell us who
they were, where they came from, or what happened to them.

9.1 The Parlour and the Cellar.

9.2 Hogarth's *Taste in High Life* shows a lady with her black boy. ▼

Property on the Run 10

Advertisements, of which only a few are shown in Figs. 10.1–10.6, tell a story of extensive resistance to slavery.

Often the same name appears month after month. Either they were block advertisements (pre-paid for a large number of insertions) or the individuals being sought found their freedom.

Where did these people go? Who sheltered them?

10.1 From the *British Apollo*, 13 February 1708.

RUN away from his Mafter on the 2d Inftant, David Marat, a Black about feventeen Years of Age, with fhort wooly Hair ; He had on a whitifh Cloath Livery, Lin'd with Blew, and Princes-mettal Buttons, with a Turbant on his Head : He founds a Trumpet, whoever fecures him and brings him to Edward Talbot Efq ; by Kingftreet near Soho, fhall have five Guines Reward.

IF any Perfon has an Eftate to difpofe of, near Reading, of about two hundred Pounds per Annum Freehold ; if fuch Perfon will apply himfelf to Mr. George Wilfon of the Middle-Temple, he may hear of a Chapman.

RUN away from his Mafter on the 14th Inftant, one Tho. Jones, about 24 Years of Age, with Pock-holes in His Face, a dark Brown Wig, in a Grey Cloath Livery lin'd with black, Stammers a little in his Speech, whoever brings him to Mr. Dikes, by the Horfe-fhooe Tavern in Drury-lane, fhall have two Guineas Reward.

A New Copy-book of Englifh, French and Italian Capitals, by Command of Hand, Price 1 Shilling. The Writing-Mafter's Affiftant enlarg'd ; and a Preface by Coll. Ayres, Price 1 Shilling 6 Pence. By Robert More. Sold by the Author, at the Golden Pen in Brownlow-Street Holborn. Where are Taught Writing, Arithmetick, Merchants Accompts and Short-hand. Alfo Youth Boarded or Taught Abroad.

LOST in or near St. Paul's Church-Yard, a green Vellum Pocket-book, with divers Receipts for Rent in it, and other Accounts; whoever has found it, and brings it to Mr. Jones in the Upper-end of St. Martins-lane, shall have ten Shillings reward, it being of no Use to any but the Owner.

RUN away from his Master on the 2d Instant, David Marat, a Black about seventeen Years of Age, with short wooly Hair; He had on a whitish Cloath Livery, Lin'd with Blew, and Princes-mettal Buttons, with a Turbant on his Head: He sounds a Trumpet, whoever secures him and brings him to Edward Talbot Esq; by Kingstreet near Soho, shall have five Guines Reward.

IF any Person has an Estate to dispose of, near Reading, of about two hundred Pounds per Annum Freehold; if such Person will apply himself to Mr. George Wilson of the Middle-Temple, he may hear of a Chapman.

10.2 From the *British Apollo*, 30 April 1708.   10.3 From the *British Apollo*, 2 June 1708.

white Hair on his Chest, his Nose and Legs motled; three Silver Bells guilt, on a blew Satten Ribon, about his Neck. Whoever has found him, and brings him to Madam Williams at Chelsea, shall have a Guinea reward, and reasonable Charges.

RUN away from his Master on the 14th Instant, one Tho. Jones, about 24 Years of Age, with Pock-holes in his Face, a dark Brown Wig, in a Grey Cloath Livery lin'd with black, Stammers a little in his Speech, whoever brings him to Mr. Dikes, by the Horse-shooe Tavern in Drury-lane, shall have two Guineas Reward.

RUN away from his Master on the 2d Instant, David Marat, a Black about seventeen Years of Age, with short wooly Hair He had on a whitish Cloath Livery, Lin'd with Blew, and Princes mettal Buttons, with a Turbant on his Head: He sounds a Trumpet, whoever secures him and brings him to Edward Talbot Esq; by Kingstreet near Soho, shall have five Guines Reward.

10.4 From the *Daily Register*, 18 October 1

ELOPED from Mr. SAMUEL DELPRATT, Merchant, at Bristol, and come to London, A NEGRO MAN, about 17 or 18 Years old, Five Feet Five or Six Inches high, had on when he left Bristol, a brown Livery Coat lined with Red, red Button Holes and Collar, red Waistcoat, a Pair of old Leather Breeches pieced at the Knee, a black Leather Cap, and a Pair of black ribbed Stockings, answers to the Name of JOHN; if he should offer to ship himself as a free Man, on Board any Ship, by directing a Line to the Jamaica Coffee House, for Capt. William Tomlinson, or to Mr. Joseph Malpas, Jeweller, in Wood Street, Cheapside, whatever Expence in stopping the said Negro shall be repaid with Thanks, and Six Guineas Reward.

TO be Sold, A Fine Lively TURTLE, in very good Condition, being just landed out of the last Ships. Enquire at the Bar of the JAMAICA Coffee House, Cornhill.

For SALE by the CANDLE,
At LLOYD's Coffee House, in Lombard Street,
THIS DAY, the 18th October,
At Twelve o'Clock at Noon,

The good Snow POLLY,

A Fast Sailer, square Stern, New England built, Burthen One Hundred and Forty Tons, more or less, having good Dimensions for the Portugal, Streights, Newfoundland, Carolina, or the Coasting Trade, is extremely well

On Thursday the 27th Instant, between Bristow Causway-hill and Stretham in Surrey, about 8 of the Clock at Night, Devereux Watson of Epsom in the County of Surrey aforesaid, was Robbed by a Highway-Man of a Bay Gelding about 14 Hands one Inch high, 6 Years old, well shaped, a little hasty at first getting upon him, his Knees formerly broke, one white Spot on the off Knee remaining, his neer Shoulder wrung with the Saddle, all bright Bay, he Gallops Trots and Paces, worth 7 or 8 l Whoever brings or sends him to Devereux Watson at Epsom, or Mr. Walkers at the Star-Inn at Chairing-Cross, shall receive 10 s. Reward, and reasonable Charges.

Wm Jacobs, a Negro, aged 22 Years, Run away from his Master on Tuesday last in the Evening, he is a middle-sized Man, with a Stammering Speech, hath the Mark of a Cut in his Forehead, and the Jerusalem Arms W. I. 1706, on his Left Arm. Whoever brings him to his Master, Alexander King, Surgeon of her Majesty's Ship the Rye-Galley, either on board the said Ship at Woolwich, or to his House in Lambeth-street in Goodman's-Fields, shall have a Guinea Reward; or if he will voluntarily return, he shall be pardoned.

10.5 From the *Daily Courant*, 29 March 1719.

10.6 From the *Daily Courant*, 4 March 1712.

Hannah Press, a Servant Maid of a Middle-Statur brown Complexion, a short Nose, Marked with the Small Pox, with Light coloured Gown and Petticoat with a little dirty Silver Lace at t bottom, and a Dark-coloured Riding-hood, speaking broad Somersetshir went away from her Service on Sunday Morning the second Insta about 11 a Clock, and carried with her the following Plate, One Si ver Tankard of old Standard holding above a Quart, One Silv Salver with a wrought Rim, Six Silver Forks with three Pron each, Six Spoons of German Silver, Two plain Salts, A Silver Stan for Oyl and Vinegar, Pepper and Mustard-Box, of new Standard Supposed to be gone away with one John Brown, an old Grey-hair Man and Squints, who was her Security, and said he lived at Ham mersmith. If any Person brings Intelligence either of the Serva Maid, or the Plate, or the Man, to Mr. Edward Bird at the Whi Lyon a Linnen-Drapers over-against Bullin-Court in the Stran shall have 4 Guineas Reward.

Lawyers and the Law 11

In the early 1700s slaves who were baptised as Christians considered themselves free. Slave owners did not wish this to continue, and asked the Crown law officers, Yorke and Talbot, for a judgement. Their judgement stated that slaves remained slaves whether they were Christians or not (see Fig. 11.1).

Granville Sharp was one of the few white people to write perceptively that black people were not destined to be slaves and that they didn't have to become white in order to be free (Fig. 11.2).

We are of Opinion, That a Slave by ning from the *West-Indies* to *Great itain* or *Ireland*, either with or with- : his Master, doth not become free, d that his Master's Property or Right him is not thereby determined or va- d: And that Baptifm doth not beftow edom on him, nor make any Altera- n in his Temporal Condition in thefe ngdoms. We are alfo of Opinion, t his Master may legally compel him return again to the Plantations. *n.* 14, 1729. P. *Yorke.* C. *Talbot.*

11.1 The Yorke and Talbot Judgement, *Gentleman's Magazine*, 1741, pp. 126–7.

11.2 From Granville Sharp, *Remarks*.

More information

Jack Gratus, *The Great White Lie, Slavery, Emancipation and Changing Racial Attitudes* (New York, Monthly Review Press, 1973).

12 Apprentices

Apprenticeships were of many different kinds; some led to trade, others were merely a form of cheap labour.

As you see from the cases in Fig. 12.1 and 12.2, masters went to great lengths to keep their apprentices.

October 1, 1764.

WHereas JOHN BOMAN, Apprentice to John Ibbett, Cordwainer at Potton, Bedfordshire, ran away from his said Master on Monday the 17th of September last, after having been guilty of very injurious Proceedings towards his said Master: This is to caution all Persons not to harbour or employ the said Apprentice, as they will be prosecuted as the Law directs.

The said John Bowman is about 19 Years of Age, about five Feet three Inches high, of a brown Complection, grey Eyes, round favoured, and has a sullen Countenance; had on when he went away, a dark brown cut Wig, blue surtout Coat, blue Waistcoat, and Leather Breeches.

Whoever will secure the said Apprentice, and give Notice or bring him to his said Master, shall be handsomely rewarded, with reasonable Charges, paid by me   JOHN IBBETT.

12.1 From the *London Chronicle*, 4 October 1764.

12.2 From the Kentish Gazette, 28 August 1795.

PUBLIC OFFICE, BOW STREET.
Before N. Bond, Esq.

The friends of an apprentice to a stocking-weaver at Lambeth brought the lad on Tuesday to this office to shew one of the modes of punishment adopted by the master, when the boys committed any fault.---it consisted of an iron collar, fastened round the neck by a padlock; the lad said he had worn it for above a month, and that he understood it was his master's intention he should wear it till he was out of his time. The master living in the county of Surry, Mr. Bond could not interfere in the business, but advised the parties to go to Union Hall, in the Borough. The master of the apprentice alluded to, we understand, has got between 60 and 70 boys, most of whom he has had from the different workhouses in the county of Surry.

More information

M. Dorothy George, *London Life in the Eighteenth Century* (Penguin, 1966/Peregrine, 1976).

The experience of European indentured servants in the Caribbean and N. America is dealt with in A. E. Smith, *Colonists in Bondage* (Chapel Mill, University and North Carolina Press, 1947).

Granville Sharp ~ 13
Civil Rights Lobbyist

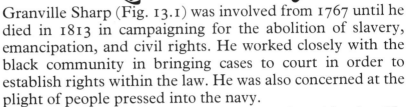

Granville Sharp (Fig. 13.1) was involved from 1767 until he died in 1813 in campaigning for the abolition of slavery, emancipation, and civil rights. He worked closely with the black community in bringing cases to court in order to establish rights within the law. He was also concerned at the plight of people pressed into the navy.

His involvement with slavery started accidently. He chanced to help a young black, Jonathan Strong, who had been beaten up and thrown out by his master. Months later, when his ex-master had him kidnapped, friends of Jonathan appealed to Sharp to help him. Sharp used the courts to get the boy freed. The news of this obviously spread throughout the black community, and it became common to turn to Sharp for help in kidnap cases. Sharp himself followed up cases as is seen from the letter (Fig. 13.2) which he wrote to Beckford concerning Beckford's advertisement (Fig. 13.3) for a runaway slave.

The extract below is part of the declaration by 'the Sons of Africa' and is a testimony of the feelings of some members of the black community, for Sharp's work:

13.1   Granville Sharp.

December 15, 1787.

Honourable and Worthy Sir,
Give us leave to say, that every virtuous man is a truly honourable man; and he that doth good hath honour to himself: and many blessings are upon the head of the just, and their memory shall be blessed, and their works praise them in the gate.

And we must say, that we, who are a part, or descendants, of the much-wronged people of Africa, are peculiarly and greatly indebted to you, for the many good and friendly services that you have done towards us, and which are now even out of our power to enumerate.

Nevertheless, we are truly sensible of your great kindness and humanity; and we cannot do otherwise but endeavour, with the utmost sincerity and thankfulness, to acknowledge our great obligations to you, and, with the most feeling sense of our hearts, on all occasions to express and manifest our gratitude and love for your long, valuable, indefatigable labours and benevolence towards us, in using every means to rescue our suffering brethren in slavery. . . .

And now, honourable Sir, with the greatest submission, we must beg you to accept this memorial of our thanks for your good and faithful services towards us, and for your humane commiseration of our brethren and countrymen unlawfully held in slavery.

And we have hereunto subscribed a few of our names, as a mark of our gratitude and love. And we are, with the greatest esteem and veneration, honourable and worthy Sir, your most obliged and most devoted humble servants.

Ottobah Cugoano	Jasper Goree
John Stuart	Gustavus Vases (Equiano)
Geo. Rob. Mandeville	James Bailey
William Stevens	Thomas Oxford
Joseph Almaze	John Adams
Boughwa Gegansmel	George Wallace

SOURCE: Prince Hoare, *Memoir of Granville Sharp* (London, 1828).

More information

Prince Hoare, *Memoir of Granville Sharp* (London, 1828).

13.2 From Prince Hoare, *Memoir of Granville Sharp.* ▼   ►

To Mr. Alderman Beckford.

(Enclosing a MS. copy of "Remarks on the Injustice of Slavery.")

" Sir,   " 17th May, 1768.

" A copy of an advertisement was put into my hands this morning, whic had been inserted in the *Daily Advertiser* of yesterday, for apprehending a poo wretched Negro boy, whereby a reward was offered to whoever will bring hin or any tidings of him, to *Mr. Beckford, in Pall Mall.* Now, Sir, as I hav a very great esteem for the name of Beckford, on account of your steady an independent behaviour on all public occasions, and because I believe you t be a sincere well-wisher to the true interests, constitution, and liberties of th kingdom, I have made bold (on a supposition that Mr. Beckford in Pall Ma may be a relation of yours) to send you the enclosed remarks, concerning th tenure of Negro Slaves in England.

" I am thoroughly persuaded that the holding of slaves in this island ma be productive of very bad consequences, especially as it seems at this time very growing evil.———I am apprehensive that you are at present of a ver different opinion, and, what is worse, I cannot at all flatter myself (notwith standing all my pains-taking) that what I have written is so far conclusive a to move your assent. Nevertheless, I hope at least that you may be thereb induced to consider the subject more seriously than you have hitherto done and on this only I rely, for I have not the least doubt, from your genera character, that, howsoever we may differ in opinion, you will, notwithstanding most certainly discard all motives of private interest, which might be liable t

ffect the point in question, if, on a strict examination, they should appear to
e repugnant to equity and justice.

Mincing Lane, 17th May, 1768.   " With the greatest respect," &c. &c.

To the Right Honourable Lord Camden, Lord High Chancellor of England.

My Lord,   " 28th November, 1769—Old Jewry.

" The enclosed advertisement (*a*) was inserted in the ' Public Advertiser' of
is day; and, as I humbly conceive that the frequency of such publications
ust tend very much to extinguish those benevolent and humane principles
hich ought to adorn a Christian nation, I hope your Lordship will pardon the
perty I now take, in laying the same before you, together with a printed
monstrance, which contains my reasons more at large.

" By the high office with which your Lordship is most worthily invested,
ou are certainly the constitutional guardian even of the meanest of his
ajesty's subjects, when oppressed; and therefore I am thoroughly persuaded
at your Lordship will take such notice of this notorious breach of the laws
nature, humanity, and equity, and also of the established law, custom, and
nstitution of England, as will be most consistent with that strict and
shaken regard for all these which has always been a distinguished part of
ur Lordship's character.

" With all imaginable respect and esteem," &c. &c.

13.3   From the *Public Advertiser*, 14 May 1768. ▼

RUN away from his Master, a
Negro Boy, under five Feet in Heighth, about
16 Years old, named **CHARLES**. He is very ill
made, being remarkably bow-legged, hollow-back'd,
and por bellied. He had on, when he went away, a
coarse dark brown Linnen **Frock**, a Thickset Waistcoat,
very dirty Leather Breeches, and on his Head an old
Velvet Jockey Cap.

Whoever will bring him, or give any Tidings of him,
to Mr. Beckford in Pall-mall, may depend upon being
very handsomely rewarded.

14 The Somerset Case

Charles Stewart left America in 1769 and came with his slave, James Somerset, to London. In 1771 James Somerset decided to escape from Stewart. He found shelter amongst London's large black population. Eventually, however, Stewart found him and had him kidnapped and sent in chains to a ship on the Thames called the *Ann and Mary*, bound for Jamaica. Somerset's friends managed to get a writ of *habeas corpus* against the ship's captain. Somerset was finally produced in court before Lord Mansfield, the Chief Justice, who referred the matter to the Court of the King's Bench for decision. Somerset's defence counsel, advised by Granville Sharp, saw this as an opportunity to challenge the legality of slavery in Britain.

Mansfield finally freed Somerset in June 1772.

The euphoria of the black community (Fig. 14.1) was short lived for the victory was only a partial one. Mansfield's judgement was merely a statement that slaves could not be taken from England by force (Fig. 14.2). He did not give a judgement on the illegality of slavery. There is no evidence which indicates that all slaves were freed. Certainly cases of kidnap and sale continued. In his own will dated 17 April 1783 Mansfield in fact freed his black niece, Dido Elizabeth Lindsay, who lived with him at Kenwood House, London.

More information

Most of F. O. Shyllon's *Black Slaves in Britain* (O.U.P., 1974), is concerned with this case and its ramifications.

On Monday near 200 **Blacks**, with their La-dies, had an Entertainment at a Public-houfe in Weftminfter, to celebrate the Triumph which their Brother Somerfet had obtained over Mr. Stuart his Mafter. Lord Mansfield's Health was echoed round the Room; and the Evening was concluded with a Ball. The Tickets for Admittance to this black Affembly were 5s. each.

14.1 From the *Public Advertiser*, 27 June 1772.

14.2 From the *Gazetteer and New Daily Advertiser*, 23 June 1772.

Yefterday the Court of King's **Bench** gave judge ment in the cafe of Somerfet the Negro, finding tha his mafter had no power to compel him on board . fhip, or to fend him back to the plantations.

Free Black Community 15

The two contrasting reports in Figs. 15.1 and 15.2 show that many black people must have been free: free to go to a late-night party, free to wander away from the inner cities and ports to the heartland of England.

15.1 From the *London Chronicle*, 16–18 February 1764.

naged. A fine outward-bound ship, deeply laden, the neareft the fhore of the fire, was in the utmoft danger. The fire began in the fail loft over the maft-yard (and not in the maft-yard) by ftoring ropes in the above loft; as it did in the fame place about 19 years ago, which then did confiderable damage in that neighbourhood.

Among the fundry fafhionable routs or clubs, that are held in town, that of the Blacks or Negro fervants is not the leaft. On Wednef-day night laft, no lefs than fifty-feven of them, men and women, fupped, drank, and enter-tained themfelves with dancing and mufic, confifting of violins, French horns, and other in-ftruments, at a public-houfe in Fleet-ftreet, till four in the morning. No Whites were al-lowed to be prefent, for all the performers were Blacks,

KALENDAR,

OF THE

PRISONERS,

In the Custody of the Keeper of the House of Correction at *Guildford* in the County of *Surrey* at the General Quarter Session of the Peace, to be holden at *Guildford*, in & for the said County, on *Tuesday* the 15th day of JULY 1783.

HENRY BOULTON Esq; Sheriff.

Remains according to former Order

Joseph Erwood, and Edward Lewis,

IMOTHY MARTIN a Negro, committed the 14th day of May 1783, by Peck Williams Esq' a loose idle and disorderly person, and charged by and on the Oath of Thomas Cooper of *Farnham* aforesaid Miller, with concealing himself behind a mill Stone in a Mill called Bourn-mill in the Parish of *Farnham* aforesaid, being under the same Roof with the Dwelling house there, with intent as he suspects to have committed a Felony therein.

2 Richard Lennagar of the Parish of *Dunsfold* committed the 22d day of May 1783, by Philip C. Webb Esq; charged on the Oath of Elizabeth Foster Single Woman, of the said Parish hath declared herself to be with child, and that the said child is likely to be born a bastard, and to be chargeable to the Parish of *Godalming*, he hath refused to give security to indemnify the said Parish for the said bastard child.

3 Mary Legg, committed the 30th day of May 1783, by Philip C. Webb Esq; charged on the Oath of Mrs. Mary Hunt Matron, of the house of Industry, in the Parish of *Whitley*, that the said Mary Legg a pauper of the said house, has Embezzled a pair of Shoes, the property of the said house, and also that she has wasted three Bushells of Flour committed to her care by the said matron, to remain two Kallender months to hard Labour.

The comment in Fig. 16.1 was typical of some later eighteenth-century press statements about race.

The number of black people already settled in Britain, combined with the exaggerated newspaper reports over the possible effects of the Somerset judgement, caused some people to demand the expulsion of the black community.

16.1 From the *London Chronicle*, 13–16 March 1773.

It is therefore humbly hoped the Parliament wlll provide fuch remedies as may be adequate to the occafion, by expelling the Negroes now here, who are not made free by their owners, and by prohibiting the introduction of them in this kingdom for the future; and fave the natural beauty of Britons from the Morifco tint; and remove the envy of our naive fervants, who have fome reafon to complain that the Negroes enjoy all the happinefs of eafe in domeftic life, while many of thofe ftarve for want of places.

More information

Eric Williams, *British Historians and the West Indies* (André Deutsch, 1972).

15.2 Kalendar of Prisoners, Surrey, 15 July 1783.

17 The Gordon Riots

The print shown in Fig. 17.1 depicts a very large crowd scene in London in 1780, and if you look carefully you can see a number of black people taking part in the general activity.

The Gordon Riots, as they became known, began as a protest to Parliament against civil rights for Catholics. The events were witnessed by Ignatius Sancho (see page 4) who lived in Westminster. He wrote in his letters:

June 6
This—this—is liberty! Genuine British liberty!—This instant about two hundred liberty-boys are swearing and swaggering by with large sticks.
Eight o'clock—Lord George Gordon has this moment announced to my Lords the mob—that the act shall be repealed this evening:—Upon this, they gave a hundred cheers—took the horses from the hackney-coach—and rolled him full jollily away:—They are huzzaing now ready to crack their throats.
June 9
The Fleet Prison, the Marshalsea, King's Bench, both Compters, Clerkenwell, and Tothill Fields, with Newgate, are all flung open; Newgate partly burned, and 300 felons from thence only let loose upon the world—Lord Mansfield's house in town suffered martyrdom; and his sweet box at Caen Wood [Kenwood] escaped almost miraculously.
Half past nine o'clock
King's Bench prison is now in flames, and the prisoners at large; two fires in Holborn now burning.

Hyde Park has a grand encampment, with artillery park, &c, &c. St. James's Park has ditto, upon a smaller scale. The Parks, and our West end of town, exhibit the features of French Government. This minute, thank God! this moment Lord George Gordon is taken, Sir F. Molineux has him safe at the Horse-Guards. Bravo! He is now going in state in an old hackney-coach, escorted by a regiment of militia and a troop of light horse, to his apartments in the Tower.

More information

*Letters of the late Ignatius Sancho,
   an African* (London, 1803),
   Letters CXXXIV–CXXXVI.
The Gordon Riots (Jackdaw
   Publications).

17.1 The Gordon Riots, 1780.

18 The Black Loyalists

During the struggle of the Americans to free themselves from British rule—the American War of Independence beginning in 1775—the British offered rewards to any Americans who would help them. For black slaves the reward was freedom. Black and white Americans who fought for Britain came to be known as Loyalists. When the British lost, the Loyalists had to leave—some went to the West Indies, others to Canada, and a third group came to Britain.

In Fig. 18.1 Lord Sydney, Prime Minister Pitt's Secretary of State, records how a new group of black people appeared in Britain. They had their freedom. Would there be any other reward for their service to Britain?

More information

Mary Beth Norton, *The British Americans: The Loyalist Exiles in England, 1774–1789* (Boston 1972, London 1974).

18.1 Lord Sydney's letter, 7 December 1786, Parliamentary Papers, 1789 (vol. 89).

N° 1. COPY of a Letter from the Right honourable Lord Sydney to the Lords Commissioners of the Admiralty dated Whitehall, 7th December 1786.

Whitehall, 7th December 1786.

My Lords,

A PLAN having been laid before the King, for sending out of this Country a Number of Black Poor (many of whom have been discharged from His Majesty's Naval Service at the Conclusion of the late War, and others after having been employed with the Army in North America) who have since their Arrival in England been reduced to the greatest Distress, in order that a Settlement may be formed in or near the River Sierra Leona, on the Coast of Africa; and His Majesty having been pleased to approve of the Plan, and in Consequence thereof to direct that Measures should immediately be taken for acquiring from the Native Chiefs a Territory of sufficient Extent for the settling of the said Black Poor, and also for furnishing them with Tools and Implements, &c. for the Cultivation of the Land as well as with Provisions for their Subsistence, until it is supposed that they will be able to raise Food for their future Support, I have received His Royal Commands to signify to your Lordships His Majesty's Pleasure, that as soon as the said Black Poor shall be embarked on Board of the Vessels which are prepared for their Reception, together with the Stores and Provisions before mentioned, you do appoint a Ship of War to escort the said Vessels to the River Sierra Leona, directing her Commander, upon his Arrival there, to give every possible Assistance to the Superintendant or Overseer who will accompany the said Black Poor in the Execution of the Plan, whilst the said Ship may remain in the said River. I shall transmit to your Lordships, as soon as may be, a Copy of the Plan, for your full Information upon this Business.

I am, &c.

SYDNEY.

Black Loyalists who came to Britain found they had freedom and little else. In common with many poor at the time, they took to street begging. The arrival of black loyalists, many of whom were forced on to the streets, reactivated 'race' phobia in some people (Fig. 19.1). Others used unemployment as an excuse to call for the expulsion of black people (Fig. 19.2).

19.1 From the *Morning Post*, 22 December 1786.

When the late Mr. Dunning was fome years ago reafoning againft making this country a refuge for all the blacks who chofe to come here, he obferved, " that the numerous dingy-coloured faces which crowded our ftreets, muft have their origin in our wives being *terrified* when pregnant, by the numerous Africans who were to be feen in all parts of the town, and if the legiflature did not take fome method to prevent the introduction of any more, he would venture to prophecy, that London would, in another century, have the appearance of an Ethiopian colony.

19.2 From the *Morning Post*, 29 December 1786.

A very popular member, it is faid, intends to bring in a bill to prevent Blacks being brought into the kingdom. There is fuch a law in France, and a very excellent one it is. When fo many of our own young men and women are out of employment, and, literally fpeaking, are ftarving in the ftreets, it is abominable that aliens, and more particularly Black aliens, fhould be fuffered to eat the bread of idlenefs in Gentlemen's houfes, &c.

20 Relief to Resettlement

The number and condition of black beggars (Figs. 20.1 and 20.2) in the streets of London caught the attention of a group of merchants, bankers and MPs. These concerned business people formed themselves into a Committee for the Relief of the Black Poor (Fig. 20.3). Public appeals for funds resulted in enough money to give daily relief in the form of broth, a piece of meat, and a twopenny loaf to each person applying. Over 200 were clothed and 50 were cared for in hospital. Relief was distributed (Fig. 20.4) at the White Raven, Mile End Road, and at Lisson Green. The number of people receiving relief rose to nearly 700.

The Committee decided, however, that the best thing for the black poor was to resettle them in Africa. They adopted Henry Smeathman's plan (Fig. 20.5) to establish a settlement on the west coast of Africa in Sierra Leone.

A proclamation (Fig. 20.6) giving details of the scheme was distributed. The project had by then been promised money from the government.

20.1.2   The names of the last men on the List of Black Poor, 1786.

20.2.1   The names of the first women on the list of Black Poor, 1786.

20.1.1   The names of the first men on the List of Black Poor, 1786.

20.2.2   The names of the last women on the List of Black Poor, 1786.

A List of the Committee for relieving the Black Poor.

JONAS HANWAY, Esq. Red Lion square, CHAIRMAN.

MONTAGU BURGOYNE, Esq. Harley Street.

B. JOHNSON, Esq. Lisson Green.

SIR JOSEPH ANDREWS, Bart. Knightsbridge.

GEORGE PETERS, Esq. Old Bethlem.

JOHN OSBORNE, Esq. New Norfolk Street.

JOHN JULIUS ANGERSTEIN, Albemarle Street.

JAMES PETER ANDREWS, Esq. Brompton.

SAMUEL HOARE, Esq. Lombard Street.

GEORGE DRAKE, Esq. Bedford Square.

. MATHEWS, Esq. Bridge Street, Westminster.

WILLIAM WARD, Esq. Fenchurch Street

RICHARD SHAW, Esq. London Bridge.

JOHN CORNWALL, Esq. Duchess Street, Portland Place.

. THORNTON, Esq. M. P. King's Arms Yard.

I. THORNTON, Esq. M. P. Bartholomew Lane.

THOMAS BODDINGTON, Esq. Mark Lane.

GENERAL MELVILLE, Brewer Street.

The Committee for the Black Poor, 1786.

PLAN

OF A

SETTLEMENT

TO BE MADE NEAR

SIERRA LEONA,

ON THE

GRAIN COAST

OF

AFRICA.

Intended more particularly for the service and happy establishment of Blacks and People of Colour, to be shipped as freemen under the direction of the Committee for Relieving the Black Poor, and under the protection of the British Government.

BY HENRY SMEATHMAN, Esq.

Who resided in that Country near Four Years.

LONDON:

Sold by T. STOCKDALE in Piccadilly, G. KEARSLEY in Fleet Street, and J. SEWEL in Cornhill.
1786.

20.5 The Smeathman Plan.

...ittee for Relief of Black Poor ⸺⸺⸺⸺⸺ Cr.

...ts for 26 Days.

1786				
June 3	By 2 Days Subsistence for 328 Persons at the Yorkshire Stingo as ⅌ Book @ 6ᵈ ⅌ Day ⸺⸺		16	8
	Arrears paid this Day to sundry Persons who had been prevented from attending regularly by Sickness or other causes		1	2
	Weekly Persons		1	8	6
	Pay Room			4	
	Edwᵈ Jackson, sick			3	
	John Lemon ⸺ dᵒ			1	
	George Brown ⸺ dᵒ			1	
5ᵗʰ	By 2 Days Subsistence for 206 Persons at the White Raven as ⅌ Book		10	6
	Arrears as above			5	
	Weekly Person			3	6

20.4 Payments List, Black Poor, 1786.

WHEREAS many Negroes and People of Colour having appeared in the Streets of London to be in great Mifery, a certain Number of Britifh Subjects did in the Beginning of the prefent Year, form themfelves into a Committee, under the Name of the Committee for the Black Poor, and afforded them fuch Relief, as the Money, collected from the Piety of their fellow Subjects, enabled them to do. **And whereas** the Right Honourable the Lords Commiffioners of the Treafury being informed of the wretched Situation of the faid Negroes and People of Colour, and the apparent Caufes thereof, have expreffed their defire that the faid Committee fhould make the neceffary Arrangements for fending the faid Blacks and People of Colour to fuch Places as they the faid Committee may think fit and proper for their profperous Eftablifhment; and their Lordfhips (as an indubitable Evidence of the Sincerity of Government) having directed the Money neceffary for this Purpofe, as far as the Rate of Fourteen Pounds of lawful Money of Great Britain per Head, to be iffued to the faid Committee for the Ufe and Service of the faid Blacks and People of Colour,

20.6 Proclamation, 1786.

The Committee used eight black men to try and persuade others to sign up to go to Sierra Leone. Each man was to try to get between a dozen and two dozen people (Fig. 21.2). The personal details of the men chosen (Fig. 21.1) are very interesting.

Names.	What Occupation	Qualification	Where Born.	Age	How came into England.
James Johnson	Husbandry	Reads	N. Jersey	31	Steward of a Ship.
Jn Wm. Ramsay	Domestic	- - - - -	N. York.	24	Do
Aaron Brookes	Husbandry	Reads & writes	N. Jersey	25	Capt's Cook of a King's Ship
John Lemon	Hairdresser & Cook	Reads.	Bengal.	29	Do
John Cambridge	Nettmaker & Domestic.	Reads	Africa	40	Domestic.
John Williams	Seaman	- - - - -	Chas Town	25	King's Ship.
Willm Green	Domestic	Reads & writes	Barbadoes	40	Domestic.
Chas. Stoddard	Cooper	Reads.	Africa	28	Do

21.1 From the Minutes of the Committee for the Black Poor, 1786. Notice the age range, occupations, areas of origin and literacy of the men on the list.

That he also attended last Monday at the White Raven at Mile End to confirm what he had said at Lisson Green; and that he had selected Eight of the most intel=ligent among the Blacks and People of Colour as Head Men, having proposed to each of them to produce a List of 12 as far as 24 Persons, as his respective Company, for whose Steddiness and good Behaviour they might be respectively answerable, as it would be otherwise impracticable to bring a confused number of such kind of Persons into such order as the nature of the Case required, for their common good. That the Persons so chosen were

James

21.2   From the Minutes of the Committee for the Black Poor, 1786.

32

Despite appeals, explanations and encouragement from the Corporals, people were taking relief but not signing up to go to Sierra Leone.

The Committee now decided on firmer action to make people sign. Relief was only to be given to those signing to go to Africa (Figs. 22.1 and 22.2).

22.1   From the Minutes of the Committee for the Black Poor, 9 October 1786.

Read an Agreement between the Blacks and Jos.^{nh} Irwin which was approved of. and it was

Resolved

That no further Money be given; but to such as sign the same.

22.2   From the Minutes of the Committee for the Black Poor, 24 October 1786.

Batson's Coffeehouse,
24.th October 1786.

Present.

Mr. Hoare
Mr. Ward
Mr. Shaw

Mr. Peters in the Chair.

Ordered

That no more money be issued to the Blacks after the 31.st Inst.

The Committee is likewise of opinion that, considering the disposition of the Blacks and their want of discipline, it may be proper that they should embark in the River near Blackwall.

23 For their own Good

The Committee had begun by appealing publicly for money to give relief. Now it wanted support of a different kind. It asked the public not to give aid to the black poor. The people who had signed would then be forced aboard the ships to go to Sierra Leone.

The Committee for the Relief of the Black Poor think it necessary to inform the Public, that three ships are now ready, amply supplied with provisions, clothing and every other necessary, in Order to establish a Free Settlement on the coast of Africa; that seven hundred have signed an engagement to go and only three hundred are on board. It being apprehended that the remainder are prevented from embarking, by the mistaken, though well intended acts of charity of individuals, in giving relief to such of the Black Poor as are still about the metropolis. The Committee submits to the consideration of the Public, whether it may not be advisable to suspend giving alms to the said persons, in order to induce them to comply with the engagement they entered into.

SOURCE: *General Evening Post*, 14–16 December, 1786.

23.1   From the *General Evening Post*,
14–16 December 1786.

The Last Resort 24

The Committee and the City authorities showed the nature of their ultimate concern for the people by trying to force them on to the ships. Signatories or not, black beggars were to be rounded up (Fig. 24.1). Despite all the pressure and inducements only 441 men, women and children finally sailed (Figs. 24.2–24.4).

24.1   From the *Public Advertiser*, 3 January 1787.

The Mayor has given orders to the City Marſhals, the Marſhalmen, and Conſtables, to take up all the blacks they find begging about the ſtreets, and to bring them before him; or ſome other magiſtrate, that they may be ſent home, or to the new colony which is going to be eſtabliſhed in Africa; near twenty are already taken up, and lodged in the two Compters.

The conduct of the Lord-Mayor in ordering the blacks who are found begging about the ſtreets to be taken up, is highly commendable, and it is to be hoped will be imitated by the Magiſtrates of Weſtminſter, Middleſex, Surry, and the other counties. It is however humbly ſubmitted to their judgment, whether inſtead of mere confinement in a gaol, it would not be preferable to put them to hard labour in Bridewell. The blacks, eſpecially thoſe of the Eaſt-Indies, are naturally indolent; nothing but the utmoſt neceſſity will make them work; and the very thought of being ſubjected to that would ſoon reconcile them to the plan propoſed by Government.

(Copy.)

Memorandum

of Agreement made the Sixth day of October In the year of our Lord One thousand seven Hundred and Eighty six And in the twenty seventh year of the Reign of His most excellent majesty King George the Third over Great Britain &c in manner and form following (that is to say) &c WE the undersigned do hereby undertake Contract and agree to and with JOSEPH Irwin (Conductor of a certain intended Settlement or Colony to be situated on the Grain Coast of Africa and to be called "The Land of Freedom"

24.2.1   Memorandum about the 'intended settlement or colony . . . to be called "The Land of Freedom" . . .'

1. John Watter Harris
2. John Wilson
3. Lewis Latouch
4. Charles Stoddart
5. William Gorman
6. John Smith
7. John William Ramsey
8. Abra.ᵐ Elliot Griffith
9. John Mandeville
10. James Strong
11.

662 John Anthony
663 Domingo Anthony
664 Thos. Sylva
665 John Oman
666 Josiah Hosier
667 John Lewis
668 John Becket
669 Eliz.ᵗʰ Williams
670 Ann Wilks
671 John Thomas Squi...
672 Fras. Steward
673 Hannah Steward
674 John Wilson
675 Thos. Freeman
676

24.2.3   The last names on the list of resettlement applicants, 1786.

24.2.2   The first names on the list of resettlement applicants, 1786.

A List of Names of W.ᵗ Black Persons embarked on board the Bellisarius Capt.ᵗ Sill. 22ⁿᵈ Nov 1786

Nᵒ
1 Will.ᵐ Hoskins
2 George Isaacs
3 Sam.ˡ Thompson
4 Alex.ʳ Thompson
5 Ja.ˢ White
6 Emanuel Saunders
7 John Steward
8 James Taylor
9 John Lawrence
10 Thomas Sims

James Neptune
25 William Richardson
    Hannah Richardson
    Edward Jones
    Francis Durham
    William Mullenden
30 George Ford
    John Aberdeen
    York Steward
    Thomas Woodman

24.3.1 The first names on the *Bellisarus* sailing list, 1786.

    Nancy Adams.
100 George Broomfield
    John Peters
    Mary Adams
    James Martin
    Barbara Thomas
105 Christopher Friday.

24.3.2 The last names on the *Bellisarus* sailing list, 1786.

List of Names of Black Persons embarked on board the Atlantic Captn Muirehead. 22nd Novr 1786

1 Anthy Smith
2 Thomas Nottingham
3 Henry Graves
4 Peter Hill
5 James Charles
6 David Draper
7 Duk Simmons
8 John Peters
9 James Titus
10 George Prince
11 James Stephenson
12 John Green
13 James Oliver

28 Thomas Clement
29 John Jupiter
30 Robert Moore
31 John Thomas
32 John Anthony
33 Susanna Thomas
34 Willm Jones
35 James Owen
36 Robt Walker
37 Thomas Nelson
38 Margt B Broughton
39 Frant B Broughton
40 Ann Cardell

24.4.1 The first names on the *Atlantic* sailing list, 1786.

145 Thomas Greer
6 Willm Green
7 Maria Green
8 B Betsey Green
9 William Green
150 Geo: Ogram
1 Cath Ogram
2 Anthy Madeira
3 Geo: Ogram
4 Elizth Horne

24.4.2 The last names on the *Atlantic* sailing list, 1786.

Two men exposed both the dangers and dishonesty of the scheme. Ottobah Cugoano obviously expressed the fears of many people in pointing out the danger of re-enslavement (Fig. 25.1).

Before the ships had left British shores Olaudah Equiano publicly exposed the mismanagement and dishonesty of the agent and his accomplices. Vital supplies, even including clothing and bedding, were not available. Olaudah was also known as Gustavus Vasa or Vassa. He signed his letter to the *Public Advertiser* (Fig. 25.2) using this alternative name.

We are sorry to find that his Majesty's Commissary for the African Settlement has sent the following Letter to Mr. John Stewart, Pall-mall:

' *At Plymouth, March* 24, 1787.

' S I R,

' These with my respects to you. I am sorry you and some more are not here with us. I am sure Irwin *, and Frafer the Parson, are great villains, and Dr. Currie. I am exceeding much grieved at the conduct of those who call themselves gentlemen. They now mean to serve (or use) the blacks the same as they do in the West Indies. For the good of the settlement I have borne every affront that could be given, believe me, without giving the least occasion, or ever yet resenting any.

' By Sir Charles Middleton's letter to me, I now find Irwin and Frafer have wrote to the Committee and the Treasury, that I use the white people with arrogance, and the blacks with civility, and stir them up to mutiny: which is not true, for I am the greatest peace-maker that goes out. The reason of this lie is, that in the presence of these two, I acquainted Captain Thomson of the Nautilus sloop, our convoy, that I would go to London and tell of their roguery; and further insisted on Captain Thompson to come on board of the ships, and see the wrongs done to me and the people: so Captain Thompson came and saw it, and ordered the things to be given according to contract—which is not yet done in many things—and many of the black people have died for want of their due. I am grieved in every respect. Irwin never meant well to the people, but self-interest has ever been his end: twice this week they have taken him, bodily, to the Captain, to complain of him, and I have done it four times.

' I do not know how this undertaking will end; I wish I had never been involved in it; but at times I think the Lord will make me very useful at last.

' I am, dear Friend,

' With respect, your's,

' G. VASA.

' The Commissary for

' the Black Poor.'

* The Agent for Africa.

25.2 From the *Public Advertiser*, 4 April 1787.

More information

O. Cugoano, *Thoughts and Sentiments on the Evil of Slavery* (London, 1787).

25.1 From O. Cugoano, *Thoughts and Sentiments on the Evils of Slavery*, (London, 1787) pp. 141–2. ▶

But some of them, by various services either to the public or to individuals, as more particularly in the course of last war, have gotten their liberty again in this free country. They are thankful for the respite, but afraid of being ensnared again; for the European seafaring people in general, who trade to foreign parts, have such a prejudice against Black People, that they use them more like asses than men, so that a Black Man is scarcely ever safe among them. Much assiduity was made use to persuade the Black People in general to embrace the opportunity of going with this company of transports; but the wiser sort declined from all thoughts of it, unless they could hear of some better plan taking place for their security and safety. For as it seemed prudent and obvious to many of them taking heed to that sacred enquiry, *Doth a fountain send forth at the same place sweet water and bitter?* They were afraid that their doom would be to drink of the bitter water. For can it be readily conceived that government would establish a free colony for them nearly on the spot, while it supports its forts and garrisons, to ensnare, merchandize, and to carry others into captivity and slavery.

26 Alternatives

Fear of enslavement stopped some people from going to Sierra Leone.

The opinions in Fig. 26.1 were offered as other reasons why some of the black poor did not accept resettlement.

26.1 From the *Morning Post*, 28 December 1786.

With refpect to thofe who have not yet embarked, I fhall fay a few words. I have queftioned all whom I could meet with in the ftreets, as to the reafon why they were backward in fulfilling the engagement to which they had put their names. The plea of two of them was this : They thought they were to be fhipped to their refpective homes. One of them does not embark for Africa, becaufe he was born at Charleftown ; the other, becaufe he is a native of Barbadoes. With refpect to the reft, they only wait until they can take many of their articles out of pawn, and extricate themfelves from the little debts which they have incurred. This was the fituation of all thofe who are now on board. The liberality of individuals has already, at the expence of fome hundreds, extricated thefe ; and Gentlemen are now endeaovuring to extend their benevolence to thofe who are eagerly waiting to experience it, and whom nothing but the want of experiencing it detains on fhore.

The Black Community 27 Threatened

The controversy over the Sierra Leone resettlement led to renewed pressure on the whole black community. There were calls in the newspapers for Britain to follow the example of the French in 1787 and pass a law to expel all black people and ban entry. As with the Somerset case, the report in Fig. 27.1 shows that the black community were organised.

27.1 From the *Morning Post*, 30 December 1786.

The oppofitionifts have converted numbers of the *black* poor into zealous *patriots*. They affembled, it feems, in Whitechapel, where they held, what the Indians term a *talk*; the purport of which was, that they had " heard of an inten- " tion of introducing the *arbitrary French laws*, " with refpect to *black people*, as part of the new " French Treaty ; and they looked upon the " *arts* now practifed to inveigle them out of a " land of liberty, with the utmoft jealoufy." In this inftance, as in many others, the lenity of our Government operates to the detriment of the nation. Are we to be told what articles in a treaty fhould be adopted or rejected, by a crew of reptiles, manifeftly only a fingle link in the great chain of exiftence above the *monkey?* Should a footy tribe of Negroes be permitted to arraign, with impunity, the meafures of Government ? A few conftables to difperfe their meetings, and a law, prohibiting *blacks* from entering our country, would be the proper mode of treating thofe crea- tures, whofe intercourfe with the inferior orders of our women, is not lefs a fhocking violation of fe- male delicacy, than difgraceful to the ftate. In France, fhould a Negroe cafually arrive, he is ef- corted to a fea-port, and difmiffed the kingdom ; and why any debafement in the *breed* of the peo- ple fhould not be an object of attention in the legiflature, a man verfed in found policy muft be at a lofs to conceive.

28 Two Way Traffic

Since 1615 many thousands of white islanders had been transported to the Americas, including the Caribbean. Some were taken as cheap labour under contracts to masters, others were kidnapped and many went as prisoners (Fig. 28.1).

Often those on the losing side in uprisings, rebellions or civil conflicts ended up being transported. After the Monmouth Rebellion in 1685, for instance, it is recorded that 329 rebels were shipped to Barbados, but only 304 lived to be sold into servitude. People convicted of criminal offences could suffer a similar fate.

The outlet to North America stopped with American independence in 1783, and the courts and authorities then considered West Africa as an alternative for convict settlement and labour (Fig. 28.2).

More information

A. E. Smith, *Colonists in Bondage* (U. of N. Carolina, 1947).

28.1 Kalendar of Prisoners, Surrey, 1785.

P R I S O N E R S

Remaining for TRANSPORTATION, &c. according to former ORDERS.

1. THOMAS ECCLES, Attainted of a burglary, was at Guildford assizes, in August, 1782 ordered to serve in his Majesty's land service, in Africa, during his natural life.

2. John Wood, Convicted of wilful and corrupt perjury, was at Guildford assizes, in August, 1782 ordered to be transported to some of his Majesty's settlements abroad, for the term of seven years.

3. John Brooker, Convicted of felony, was in January sessions, 1783, ordered to be transported to Africa, for the term of three years.

4. William Hubbard, and
5. William Bogie, } Convicted of felony, was at the adjournment of the above sessions, the 19th. of February, 1783, ordered to be transported to some of his Majesty's colonies in America, for the term of seven years.

6. James Harris, Convicted of felony, was at the same adjournment, the 19th. of February, 1783, ordered to be transported to Africa, for the term of fourteen years.

7. John Garrick, Attainted of felony, was at Kingston assizes, the 19th. of March, 1783, ordered to serve in his Majesty's land service, abroad, during his natural life.

8. Robert Hamblin, and
9. William Shera, } Convicted of grand larceny, was at Kingston assizes, the 19th. of March, 1783, ordered to be transported to some of his Majesty's settlements in Africa, for the term of three years each.

The Reason why the persons first named are to be sent to Africa is this they are notorious Felons who were every Day expected to break prison some of them had (I am informed) made attempts to do it & are a Class of People too dangerous to remain in this Country & it was thought there was no proper Place in America to transport them to at least within the Kings Dominions

29 Too Great a Risk

Convicts were sent to Africa. In 1782, 350 were sent (Fig. 29.2). They were used as soldiers on the slave forts on the West African coast. These forts were huge jails where slaves were kept before being shipped across the Atlantic. The convicts didn't like being jailers. Many ran off into the countryside. Others caused a great deal of trouble to the authorities.

The attitude of the convicts posed a real threat to the smooth running of the slave trade (Fig. 29.1).

The documents were part of the evidence heard in 1785 by the Committee trying to find places to which to send convicts.

The combination of convicts and Africans was too great a risk, and Australia was considered a safer place for convict settlement.

29.2 Parliamentary Committee on Convict Transportation, 1786. ▶

More information

C. Blainey, *The Tyranny of Distance* (Macmillan, 1968) examines the early history of convict settlements.

29.1 Parliamentary Committee on Convict Transportation, 1786.

What do you think would be the Consequence of sending out a Colony of Men without Women? They would marry with the Natives who will readily part with the Women if any presents could be made of any Trifling Sum

Mr Street a Member examined

I went to Africa in 1782
with the Leander alligator and the
Zephyr Sloop in Company with
the Mackarel Transport with
350 Convicts on board her which
were carried to Cape Coast Castle
they were enlisted as Troops and
were under Military Discipline
with proper Officers — they were
allowed provisions

During the Voyage

30 Crown Service

The three prints in Figs. 30.1, 30.2 and 30.3 show that black people served in Britain's armed forces in the late eighteenth and early nineteenth centuries.

30.2   *Greenwich 1830*, engraving by Croce. ▶

30.1   The *Death of Nelson*, engraving by C. W. Sharpe.

30.3   Chelsea Pensioners receiving news of the victory at Waterloo.

31 Aftermath

The end of the Napoleonic wars in 1815 saw many soldiers and sailors returning to England and seeking re-employment.

Many were unable to do so and tried to earn a living by wandering round the country begging. Vagrants, as they were called, were found everywhere and many ended up in court.

Record of Quarter Sessions, Shropshire, 1820–30

Vagrants

1820 April   Joseph Carter, aged 26, to St. Thomas, West Indies. James Camden, aged 27, born Martinique, to North Shields.

1820 July   James Scott, aged 26, born Egypt, to Glasgow.

1821 January   Juan Buntish Cora, aged 24, born Cuba, found in Wembs Wild.

1821 July   Armagh Carrantha, aged 20, born Isle de France, East Indies, found in Drayton.
John Burton, aged 26, born St. Kitts, West Indies, found in Adderly.

SOURCE: Shropshire Records Office.

The streets of London were again populated by large numbers of beggars who troubled the conscience of the rich (Fig. 32.1).

They were classified by the authorities according to where they were born in Great Britain or whether they were of foreign origin (Fig. 32.2). The British poor were sent back to the parishes they came from because it was the responsibility of those parishes to support them.

In order to stop 'undeserving' beggars getting help, an organisation called the Society for the Suppression of Mendicity was established (Fig. 32.3). Two of its Committee had been on the 1786 Committee for Relieving the Black Poor. They were S. Thornton, M.P. and M. Burgoyne.

Instead of people giving money to beggars, the organisation sold cards which could be given instead. The beggars were then supposed to take them to the Mendicity office. There they were questioned and records checked. If they were thought deserving, they were given help. Those thought undeserving were prosecuted and punished as impostors.

Parliament responded to demands to deal with the nationwide problem of vagrancy by passing, in 1824, a Vagrancy Act. This Act made it possible for any person suspected of loitering with intent to commit a crime to be arrested and charged as a suspected person.

Figs. 32.4 and 32.5 give reports of a selection of cases dealt with by the Mendicity Society.

32.1 A black beggar, 1815, from *The Streets of London* (J. T. Smith, 1854).

32.2 A classification by the Society for the Suppression of Mendicity of black beggars according to where they were born (the first two groups refer to beggars born in England).

To parishes in London	845
To parishes in the Country	1305
Persons who did not know where they were born, and without settlements	224
Irish	1561
Scotch	201
Welch	220
French	23
Germans	32
Russians	18
Austrians	2
Prussians	13
Spaniards	21
Portuguese	9
Italians	18
Isle of Guernsey	5
Isle of Jersey	3
Holland	14
Swedes	25
Africans	46
Asiatics	28
Americans	69
Total	**4682**

Of whom 117 were Black.

SOCIETY

FOR THE

SUPPRESSION OF MENDICITY,

ESTABLISHED IN LONDON MARCH 25, 1818.

SUPPORTED BY VOLUNTARY CONTRIBUTIONS.

Patron:
HIS ROYAL HIGHNESS THE DUKE OF YORK.

President:
HIS GRACE THE DUKE OF NORTHUMBERLAND.

Vice Presidents:

DUKE OF GRAFTON	LORD LILFORD
MARQUIS OF ANGLESEA	Rt. Hon. N. VANSITTART, M.P.
EARL OF DARTMOUTH	Rt. Hon. C. ARBUTHNOT, M.P.
EARL OF HARDWICKE	Rt. Hon. W. S. BOURNE, M.P.
EARL OF CHICHESTER	Hon. GEORGE VERNON
EARL OF VERULAM	S. THORNTON, Esq. M.P.
EARL GROSVENOR	I. DRUMMOND, Esq.
EARL SHEFFIELD	JAS. BULLER, Esq.
LORD BROWNLOW	J. WEYLAND, Jun. Esq.
LORD DYNEVOR	MATTHEW MARTIN, Esq.
LORD CALTHORPE	

Visitor: M. MARTIN, Esq.——*Treasurer:* W. WILLIAMS, Esq. M.P.

Board of Management for 1818

Wm. ALLEN, Esq.	Wm. FREND, Esq.	H. POWNALL, Esq.
C. BARCLAY, Esq.	T. P. FORSTER, Esq.	Rev. Dr. RANDOLPH
H. BLAIN, Esq.	H. B. GASCOIGNE, Esq.	M. ROBINSON, Esq.
Rev. B. BURGESS	J. HARRISON, Esq.	D. RICARDO, Esq.
M. BURGOYNE, Esq.	J. HUME, Esq. M.P.	T. ROWCROFT, Esq.
P. COLQUHOUN, Esq. LL. D.	C. HUNT, Esq.	Rev. J. RUDGE
	J. T. HOPE, Esq.	JOHN SMITH, Esq.
Rev. A. CAMPBELL	J. KINGSTON, Esq.	W. TOOKE, Esq. F.R.S.
J. CLARKE, Esq.	J. MILLAR, Esq.	Rev. J. TOWERS
C. FRANCIS, Esq.	M. MARTIN, Jun. Esq.	R. WILBRAHAM, Esq.
J. FREESE, Esq.	M. PHILLIPS, Esq.	I. L. WILLIAMS, Esq.

Auditors:
A. CORBETT, Esq.—J. D. COLLIER, Esq.—J. WARREN, Esq.

Honorary Counsel:	*Honorary Solicitor:*
JOSEPH GREEN WALFORD, Esq.	WILLIAM TOOKE, Esq. F.R.S.
Honorary Secretary:	*Assistant Secretary*
Mr. WILLIAM HENRY BODKIN.	Mr. BEZER BLUNDELL.

Constables:

CHARLES DEARING	JOHN BANES
CURTIS CROFTON	WALTER STEEL
JOHN WRIGHT	ELISHA BICKLE
GEORGE JACKSON	HENRY STANTON.

Register Clerk: Mr. KEMSHEAD.——*Clerk of Inquiry:* Mr. E. R. MIVART.

Clerk: Mr. JOHN FAGAN.——*Collector:* Mr. JOHN STEPHENS.

SOCIETY'S HOUSE,

No. 13, RED LION SQUARE, HOLBORN.

Office Hours,—Nine to Six o'Clock.

32.3   Officers of the Society for the Suppression of Mendicity.

No. 4132.—J. W. M. aged fifty-eight, a native of Jamaica, was apprehended begging and taken before a Magistrate, who ordered him to be searched, when a quantity of meat, vegetables and money were found upon him. It appeared that he had before been imprisoned for the same offence, and was therefore committed to the Sessions. Soon after his liberation, he was again apprehended by the Society's officers, but refused to come to the office; upon being taken before the Magistrate, he was again committed to the Sessions, and upon being prosecuted by the Society, was sentenced to be imprisoned six months, and well flogged.

No. 4144.—M. M. a native of Ireland, with three children, applied for relief, stating herself to be in much distress; that she was very ill, her husband out of work, and the Overseers of the parish in which she resided allowed her but three shillings per week. Money and food was given her. Last winter she again applied, with her husband; work was offered him at eight pence per day, with food for himself and family, which this man absolutely refused, although he had nothing whatever to do,) saying he could provide for his family much better by begging.

32.4   Case studies of beggars, Society
for the Suppression of Mendicity.

More information

Reports of the Society for the
  Suppression of Mendicity
  (London, 1819 onwards).

No. 5403.—J. P. a young man of colour, native of Maryland, at which place he was a gentleman's servant; and having leave to go to Virginia, the place was taken possession of by the English Army, and he with many others were made prisoners, and put on board the Wezer, which sailed for the West Indies; he afterwards went to New Orleans, where he procured a situation with Capt. W——, with whom he came to England, but being discharged, was unable to procure any situation, having only a written character. The Society employed him as a messenger, in which situation he conducted himself with great propriety for several months, when one of the Managers engaged him as footman, and he was supplied with clothes and other necessaries at the expense of the Society.

No. 5419.—M. S. a decent looking young woman, with a child, had gained a settlement in Worcestershire. Having lost her husband, she was left with an afflicted child without any visible means of support. An application was made by the Society to the parish, and a weekly allowance obtained; whilst this was pending she was relieved with food and lodging, and having a good character, several articles were redeemed from pawn; the child continued very ill for a long time, during which she was frequently assisted, being totally prevented from getting a livelihood: the child is now dead, and she has obtained a situation. A very ample supply of clothing has been given her.

32.5 Case studies of beggars, Society for the Suppression of Mendicity.

33.1 *Noon*, engraving by Hogarth, 1738.

HERE
Lieth the Body of
SCIPIO AFRICANUS
Negro Servant to y Right
Honourable Charles William
Earl of Suffolk and Bradon
who died y 21 December
17 20 Aged 18 Years

I who was Born a PAGAN and a SLAVE
Now Sweetly Sleep a CHRISTIAN in my Grave
What tho' my hue was dark my SAVIOR'S sight
Shall Change this darkness into radiant light
Such grace to me my Lord on earth has given
To recommend me to my Lord in heaven
Whose glorious second coming here I wait
With saints and Angels Him to celebrate

33.2   Scipio Africanus's tombstone,
Henbury Parish Church, Bristol.

3.3 Memorial to Anna Vassa, Chesterton Parish Church, Cambridge.

Near this Place lies Interred
ANNA MARIA VASSA,
Daughter of GUSTAVUS VASSA the AFRICAN.
She died July 21. 1797.
Aged 4 Years.

Should simple village rhymes attract thine eye,
Stranger, as thoughtfully thou passest by,
Know that there lies beside this humble stone
A child of colour haply not thine own:
Her father born of Afric's sun-burnt race,
Torn from his native fields, ah foul disgrace;
Through various toils, at length to Britain came
Espous'd, so Heaven ordain'd, an English dame,
And follow'd Christ; their hope two infants dear.
But one, a hapless Orphan, slumbers here.
To bury her the village children came,
And dropp'd choice flowers, and lisp'd her early fame;
And some that lov'd her most as if unblest,
Bedew'd with tears the white wreath on their breast:
But she is gone and dwells in that abode
Where some of every clime shall joy in God.

3.4 *A Milling Match* from Cruikshank's series 'Life in London', engraving by Elmes.

33.5 *A Milling Match*, engraving by T. Rowlandson.

33.6 *The Veterans*, engraving by Thomas Jones.

T. Jones. Fecit.

THE VETERANS,

"Then broach a Can before we part.
A friendly one with all our Heart!"

Diarists and chroniclers commented on the existence of the black community in London in the 1800s.

Cruickshank produced a series of drawings called 'Life in London'. His *Lowest 'Life in London'* (Fig. 34.1) has the character of a caricature but clearly relied on contemporary evidence.

An American, Professor B. Silliman, recorded his impressions in 1806:

> A few days since I met in Oxford Street a well dressed white girl who was of ruddy complexion and even handsome, walking arm in arm and conversing very sociably with a negro man who was as well dressed as she and so black that his skin had a kind of ebony lustre. As there are no slaves in England, perhaps the English have not learned to regard negroes as a degraded class of men, as we do in the United States, where we have never seen them in any other condition.

SOURCE: B. Silliman, *A Journal of Travels in England, Holland and Scotland, 1805–1806*, 3rd ed., 1820.

34.1   *Lowest 'Life in London'*, drawn and engraved by Cruikshank.

35 Ira Aldridge

Ira Aldridge (Fig. 35.1) was a well-known and very talented actor. He performed in famous theatres in towns and cities throughout Britain and Europe. His talent was recognised by newspaper drama critics and fellow actors. Despite this, some individuals and the pro-slavery merchants in London tried to prevent him acting. These people showed basic racial prejudice by objecting to Ira Aldridge, a black actor, touching Ellen Tree, a white actress. During his first London appearance in 1825 at the Coburg Theatre (now the famous Old Vic) he met and married Margaret Gill, who came from Northallerton in Yorkshire.

During his tours of Britain he acted at the Theatres Royal in Liverpool, Manchester, Bristol, Bath and Dublin. In London he performed at the Theatre Royal, Covent Garden, the Lyceum, and the Haymarket. His performances included playing King Lear, Macbeth, Shylock and Othello.

Although he lived at Upper Norwood, South London, some of his greatest successes came from his continental tours. After performing in Germany, France, Switzerland, Austro-Hungary and Russia, he was given medals and honours in all these places.

At the age of 56 in 1863 he became a British citizen, and his wife, Margaret, died the year after. He was then married to a Swedish opera singer, Arian da Pauline Brandt, but during yet another continental tour he died in Poland. He was buried at Lodz on 7 August 1867.

Ira Aldridge had four children. Three of them were musical and his namesake daughter, Ira Montagu Ring Aldridge, trained with the Swedish singer, Jenny Lind, and herself became a composer and singing teacher in Kensington.

35.1 Ira Aldridge.

More information
Herbert Marshall and Mildred Stock, *Ira Aldridge : The Negro Tragedian* (London, 1958).

William Cuffay 36

William Cuffay (Fig. 36.1) was a leading member of the group known as the Chartists. They fought for political rights for working men, including the right to vote.

William was born in 1788 on board a ship coming to England from St. Kitts in the West Indies. His father was a slave born on the island of St. Kitts and his grandfather had been taken there from Africa.

In England the family were free. William's father became a cook on a warship and the family settled in Chatham, Kent.

William became a journeyman tailor and was increasingly involved in politics. In 1840 he was elected as a delegate from Westminster to the Chartists Metropolitan Delegate Council.

In 1848 he was elected as a member of the National Chartist Convention. Arrest soon followed and he was sentenced to transportation for life.

In Tasmania he continued to work for political rights and by the time of his death in 1870 had earned the respect of the Tasmanian community.

36.1   William Cuffay, from *Reynolds's Political Instructor*, 13 April 1850.

37 Mary Seacole

Two famous women were involved in the Crimean War. They both became famous on their return to London in 1857. One, Nurse Florence Nightingale, has been well remembered to this day; the second, Nurse Mary Seacole (Fig. 37.1), has been almost forgotten.

Mary Seacole served in the thick of the fighting and helped the wounded and dying at the assault on Redan, the Battle of Tchernaya and the fall of Sebastopol. Many of the British troops who were not wounded in the war were suffering from cholera. Mary had already spent three years nursing cholera sufferers in Panama and had suffered a slight form of the disease herself. She was well qualified to help them.

Mary was born in Jamaica in 1805 and had always wanted to be a nurse. She helped her mother nurse British soldiers there, and also spent three years in Britain. She helped during the yellow fever outbreak in Jamaica in 1853.

When Mary Seacole heard that troops she had helped in Jamaica had gone to the Crimea, she decided to go there too. On arriving in London no officials would give her any assistance to get to the Crimea. She paid for herself to go. At the end of the war she came back to London. She was now famous but poor. Many military men now came to her aid. A four-day music festival—with over a thousand performers, nine military bands and an orchestra—was held in London's Surrey Gardens to raise funds for her.

She wrote her life story in 1857 entitled *The Wonderful Adventures of Mrs. Seacole in Many Lands*. She died on 14 May 1881 and in her will left bequests to Queen Victoria's nephew, Count Gleichen, and to Lord Roseberry. She was buried at St. Mary's Cemetery, Harrow Road, London.

37.1 Mary Seacole.

More information

J. Elise Gordon, 'Mary Seacole—A Forgotten Nurse, Heroine of the Crimea', *The Midwife, Health Visitor and Community Nurse*, vol. ii, February 1975.

Samuel Coleridge-Taylor 38

Coleridge-Taylor (Fig. 38.1) is most famous for his musical composition *Hiawatha's Wedding Feast*. He composed many other works for orchestra, piano and organ, and he was a conductor at festivals in Britain and the U.S.A.

Samuel was born in Holborn in 1875 and lived most of his life in Croydon. He faced much colour prejudice and abuse which he opposed all his life. As an adult he wrote many letters to the newspapers arguing that he considered himself the equal of any white man who ever lived and no one could ever change his mind in that respect. He was deeply interested in black identity and his works *An African Suite* and *Touissant L'Ouverture* were amongst others an indication of this.

Samuel's father was an African from Sierra Leone and his mother was English. His father returned to Africa after becoming a member of the Royal College of Surgeons.

Samuel married and had two children. His daughter, Avril Coleridge-Taylor, also became a conductor and composer. She has had her own orchestra and singing group, has conducted her father's music at the Royal Albert Hall, and conducted the BBC Symphony Orchestra. His son lives in South London.

38.1   Samuel Coleridge-Taylor.

More information

W. C. Borwick Sayers, *Samuel Coleridge-Taylor—Musician : His Life and Letters* (London, 1915).
Avril Coleridge-Taylor, *The Heritage of Samuel Coleridge-Taylor* (Dobson, 1979).

39 Dr. Ernest Goffe

Ernest Goffe (Fig. 39.1) was born in Port Maria, Jamaica on 12 September 1867, the youngest son of a merchant and planter. His family had come to Jamaica from Barbados in 1823. The family claim (without positive proof) to be descended from one of Cromwell's major-generals—William Goffe—who signed King Charles I's death warrant.

Ernest Goffe came to London in 1889 to study medicine at University College Hospital. A keen sportsman, he was *victor ludorum* (games champion) at the hospital, played Rugby for Rosslyn Park and was a referee for the new sport of women's hockey. He was a member of the Fabian Society, a group later attached to the Labour Party. After qualifying as a doctor he worked as a G.P. and at St. Ann's General Hospital (earlier called the North Eastern Fever Hospital), Tottenham, where in the First World War he treated many wounded soldiers.

After the war Dr. Goffe and his wife became G.Ps. in Kingston-on-Thames and in addition he performed many operations at the local Victoria Hospital. His son, Alan, also became a doctor (and games champion) at University College Hospital. Alan was one of the research team that developed the Sabin polio vaccine which today protects many children. Dr. Ernest Goffe worked into his eighties and died shortly after retiring.

39.1 Dr. Ernest Goffe (centre) and colleagues at the North Eastern Fever Hospital, Tottenham.

Councillor J.R. Archer 40

John Archer was elected Mayor of Battersea, London, in 1913. Newspapers highlighted the story as can be seen from the *Daily Express* report in Fig. 40.2.

John came to Battersea from Liverpool as a student, set up his own photography business at 214 Battersea Park Road, and lived there until he died in 1931, aged 68 years.

He took an interest in local politics and served as a councillor for over twenty years. Besides his year as mayor (Fig. 40.1), he served on eleven council committees, took a particular interest in health and Poor Law affairs, and was a governor of several local schools.

He devoted a lot of time to being secretary and agent of the North Battersea Divisional Labour Party and deputy leader of the Labour Group on the borough council.

John Archer was very proud to have been Britain's first black Mayor.

Mayor John Archer can be ... in the lower left of this ...tograph from the *Daily Graphic*, ...nuary 1914.

'BLACK' MAYOR OF BATTERSEA.

SPEECH IN DEFENCE OF HIS COLOUR AND RACE.

WORLD'S RECORD.

For the first time, it is believed, in the history of local government, a man of colour was yesterday elected mayor of an English borough. He was Mr. John Richard Archer, who, by the solid vote of the Progressive party—numbering thirty to the Municipal Reformers' twenty-nine—was chosen Mayor of Battersea.

No reference was made in the speeches preceding the election by either side to Mr. Archer's race.

"It is a victory such as has never been gained before," said the new mayor in his opening speech to the council. "I am the proud victor. I am a man of colour. Many of the things that have been said about me, however, are absolutely untrue.

"I have a brother, but I should have to have several for us to be born in as many places as we have been said to have been born in."

"Where were you born?" interjected a councillor.

"I think," said the mayor, "that at least you ought to show me, after my election, the same respect as you would show a white man. I have been charged with not being of the superior race, and it behoves you now to show that you do belong to the superior race.

"I am the son of a man born in the West Indian Islands. I was born in England, in a little obscure village probably never heard of until now—the city of Liverpool. I am a Lancastrian bred and born.

"My mother—well, she was my mother. My mother was not born in Rangoon. She was not Burmese. She belonged to one of the grandest races on the face of the earth. My mother was an Irishwoman.

"So there is not so much of the foreigner about me after all.

"I must compliment the Press on the manner in which it has conducted this campaign. There has not been a single word to which I could take objection. They have said I am a man of colour. I am. I am proud to be. I would not change my colour if I could.

"There appeared, however, in the 'South-Western Star' a letter written by a gentleman who claims to represent the majority of the people of Battersea, yet has not the courage to sign his own name. He adopts the nom de guerre of 'True Progressive.'

"'It is not meet,' he says, 'that white men should be governed and controlled by a man of colour.'"

"Hear, hear," interjected a councillor.

"'It has always been that the white man has ruled,' the writer continues, 'and it always must be so. If not, good-bye to the prestige of Great Britain.'

"'"East is East,"' he quotes, '"and West is West, but never the twain shall meet."'

"I will reply with a saying far older than that: 'And God hath made of one blood all the nations of the earth.'

"Is it true that 'East is East and West is West, and never the twain shall meet'? Why, not so long ago you were breaking your necks to put the wedding ring on the finger of the East—to make an alliance with Japan.

"You were very glad to ally yourselves with Japan, and you only enter into an alliance—not with inferiors—but with people you think your equals.

"I have to pay the same rates and taxes as you.

"My critic probably calls himself an Imperialist. How can you be an Imperialist if not in taking in people of my colour? That kind of man is an Imperialist when he wants more land; but when an Indian or a negro comes over here he ceases to be 'Imperialist,' and becomes 'True Progressive.'

"I shall be glad to know if a man born under the Union Jack, whoever he be, has not the same rights as the white man. The colour of the skin cannot alter the affection of the heart.

"My election to-night marks a new era. You have made history. For the first time in the history of the English nation a man of colour has been elected mayor of an English borough.

"That will go forth to all the coloured nations of the world. They will look to Battersea and say, 'It is the greatest thing you have done. You have shown that you have no racial prejudice, but recognise a man for what you think he has done.'"

Reference was made in the earlier speeches to the social duties which will devolve on the new mayor and his wife. These will include attendance at many Mansion House functions, and it is a general custom for London mayors to be presented at Court.

MR. AND MRS. J. R. ARCHER.

Peace and War

In the nineteenth century Britain had a world-wide empire. All the people living within it were British subjects. Some travelled to Britain as seamen and settled in ports like Cardiff, Liverpool, Glasgow and London. Like all seamen they were often on the move.

The list of names in Fig. 41.1 is taken from London seamen's registers dated 1870 and 1912.

During the First World War more merchant seamen were needed. The photograph in Fig. 41.2 shows the crew of a British ship in 1916.

These men faced the hazard of U boat attacks as the Germans tried to stop food and supplies getting to Britain. Thousands of sailors died during these attacks but the men listed in Fig. 41.3 managed to survive.

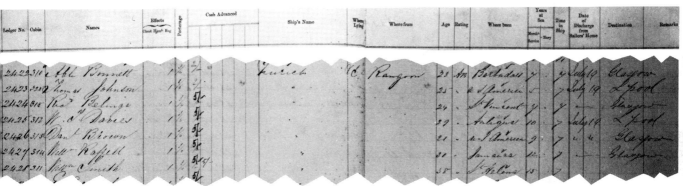

41.1.1   From the Seamen's Register, 14 July 1870, Sailor's Home and Red Ensign Club Collection.

41.1.2   Seamen's Register, 5 June 1912.

41.1.3   Seamen's Register, 19 November 1912.

◀ 40.2   From the *Daily Express*, 11 November 1913.

GROUP OF MEMBERS
OF THE CREW OF H.M. MESSENGER SHIP TRENT.

41.3.1 Seamen's Register, 18 June 1917. ▼

Date of Entry	Ledger No.	Cabin	Names &	Effects C	B		Ship's Name	Dock	Where from	Age	Rating	Where Born	Time in Ship	Remarks	Destination
	550	27	G. D. Telfer (Multey)				Elsinore	Medit	Torpedoed	17	Boy	S. Shields	Shipping Fed	19/6 refer to E. Fa.	
	551	17	H. Washington				"	"	"	23	Fm	Jamaica		" "	"
	552	4	Jas. Barrington				"	"	"	39	Fm	Barbadoes		" "	"
	553	2	C. J. Griffiths				"	"	"	52	Cook	Chester		" "	"
	554	2	James Morgan				"	"	"	29	Fm	Jamaica		" "	"
	555	2	Henry Neil				"	"	"	26	Fm	"		" "	"
	556	2	John James				"	"	"	33	Fm	Sierra Leone		" "	"
	557	2	John Henry				"	"	"	31	Fm	St. Kitts		" "	"
	558	109	10	John Williams				"	"	"	24	Fm	Sierra Leone		" "	"
	559	114	10	J. Christian				"	"	"	28	Fm	Jamaica		" "	"
	2017			J. Goldfinch						"	25	Fm	Sierra Leone		For Feb	
	2018	53	2	M. Silver				"			20	Fm	Portugal			
	2019	30	2	J. Wilson				"				Fm				
	2020			G. Turner				"		"	22	Fm	Alabama		For Feb	
	2021		10	M. Conroy				"			26	Fm	Portugal		do	
	2022		2	S. Vilano				"			25	Fm	Brazil			
	2023			M. Nicholas				"			31	Fm	St Vincent		For Feb	
	2024	148	12	F. Hansen				"			36	Cook	W. Indies			
	2025			F. Glasgow				"			19	2 Cook	W. Africa			
	2026			L. Purcay				"			21	Room mess	S. America		For Feb	

41.3.2 Seamen's Register, 28 November 1917. ▲   41.3.3 Seamen's Register, 25 January 1918. ▼

Jan 22	2474	10	Wm. Bennett	Suit Sunton 76/	Serrana	Poole	Torpedoed	Barbados		
	2475	10	August Argle	"	"	"	"	"		
	2476	10	Gordon Duke	"	"	"	"	"		
	2477	10	Samuel Jackman	"	"	"	"	Trinidad		
	2478	10	John Morris	Passengers room w/c 2 day only	"	"	"	Demarara	9/- Paying own w/c 2 days till 8th Monday	
	2479	10	John Smith	"	"	"	"	Barbados		
	2480	10	Edmond Fergus	"	"	"	"	St Lucia		
	2481	10	Samuel Workman	"	"	"	"	Barbados		
	2482	10	Garfield Agard	"	"	"	"	"		
	2483	10	Wm. Ford	"	"	"	"	"		
	2484	10	James Allman	"	"	"	"	Demarara		
	2485	10	St. Clair Smith	"	"	"	"	Barbados		

Answering the Call 42
'For King and Country'

Public meetings were held throughout the empire encouraging people in the war effort.

The photograph in Fig. 42.1 was taken in Port of Spain, Trinidad in 1916.

People from the West Indies, India and Africa, as well as from Australia, New Zealand and Canada, fought for Britain all over the world.

Fig. 42.2 shows the second contingent of British West Indian troops leaving Kingston, Jamaica, in January 1916. The troops pictured in Fig. 42.3 were members of the West Indies regiment in Belgium.

At the end of the war many troops came to Britain. They stayed in camps like the one at Pitt Corner, Winchester. You can read about the celebrations in which they took part in Figs. 42.4, 42.5 and 42.6.

42.1   Recruiting scene in Trinidad, 1916.

42.2 Kingston, Jamaica, January 1916.

42.3 West Indian troops, Albert-Amiens Road, 1916.

EMPIRE DAY IN WINCHESTER.

AT PITT CORNER CAMP.

The very picturesque camp at Pitt Corner was the scene of Empire Day festivities for the Bermuda Artillery and British West Indians. A very appetising repast had been prepared in the open air by Lieut. Preece and his staff of workers, and the feast was preceded by a stirring address on "Empire Day" by the Rev. Canon Braithwaite. "The first Empire Day," he said, " since the cessation of hostilities, when we emerged victorious from the floods of war that threatened at one time to overwhelm the British Empire will long be remembered by us. Here in view of the ancient capital of England and near the Cathedral beneath which lie the bones of many famous old English Kings— we meet together brothers drawn from far-distant parts of our world-wide Empire. You needed no conscription, but came forward voluntarily from the Bermudas and the West Indies, and I come here to-day as a Britisher to thank you most heartily for all you have done for the Empire in this world war." The tables were decorated with various kinds of wild flowers which grow in great profusion in the neighbourhood.

The afternoon was devoted to sports of an amusing character, and during the afternoon a visit was paid to the camp by Major-General Douglas Smith, G.O.C. Portsmouth Area, attended by Brig.-Gen. Macpherson and Col. Richardson, of the Repatriation Camp.

In the evening a concert was given in the Y.M.C.A. by Miss Brown's Concert Party from Eastleigh, and there were also musical selections by the Royal Munster Fusiliers' band.

42.4   From the *Hampshire Observer*, 31 May 1919.

More information

General C. Lucas; *The Empire at War*, Vols. 1–5, (O.U.P., 1923).

THE PART OF THE COLONIES.

Dauntlessly, tirelessly, they accomplished their purpose, and the world, strengthened and equipped for worthier deeds and a nobler life than any yet known, was hallowed above all by the sacrifice now commemorated in thankfulness and prayer. Thousands of stalwart men from Canada and the vast lands under the Southern Cross had unflinchingly laid down their lives, and we reverently paid our tribute of thanksgiving.

The Colonies had always shared our history, but now they had made a history of their own, and when men told in centuries to come of Gallipoli, Vimy Ridge, Villers-Bretonneux, and Ypres, it would be for the indomitable prowess and selfless devotion of the men of Canada, Australia, New Zealand, South Africa, and Newfoundland that they would thank God.

42.5   From *The Times*, 26 May 1919.

THE MEN FROM THE ENDS OF THE EARTH.

TRIBUTE TO "SOLITARY HEROES."

A special service of thanksgiving and remembrance for soldiers from oversea was held, at the desire of the Overseas Club and Patriotic League and West Indian Contingent Committee, in the church of St. Clement Danes.

Bishop Frodsham, formerly of North Queensland, Canon Residentiary of Gloucester, delivered an address, and the Rev. F. W. T. Elliott, formerly Archdeacon of Berbice, British Guiana, also took part in the service. The church was beautifully decorated with flags and flowers—red, white, and blue. Special arrangements had also been made for the musical side of the service. The choir was augmented, and the Australian Imperial Force sent its band. The congregation contained representatives not only of all the Dominion troops, but also of troops from the West Indies and volunteers from South America.

Bishop Frodsham, in his address, said that there was no part of the whole earth from which men had not come to fight for the Empire. Honour to whom honour was due; yet in honouring the men from oversea it was necessary to preserve proper proportion. To speak as though they had borne the sole burden of the war, or even had done more than the rest to preserve the treasures of Empire, would be repugnant to the men themselves. Those who had walked in the fiery furnace did not talk lightly of their own prowess. Neither did they desire to minimize the prowess of others.

The main burden of the war had fallen upon the men of these islands, and particularly upon the English regiments, who with magnificent humility had fought everywhere and everywhere given the praise to others. This the men from oversea would be the first to acknowledge, while the American troops, by joining in the Empire celebrations, were showing the same generous spirit of comradeship.

There were some from oversea to whom no State laid claim. These masterless men heard the call of the Empire on the South American pampas, on the coral strands of the Pacific Islands, in the jungles of Africa, in all the five continents and on all the seven seas. Having heard the voice of duty, they were not disobedient to it. These did not clamour for exemption or for safe appointments. Commissioners and planters, sailors and stockmen, rich and poor alike, they were content to enlist as men, to fight as men, to suffer like men, and, when occasion demanded it, to die like men. When honour was given, let no man forget the solitary heroes of Empire.

42.6   From *The Times*, 26 May 1919.

43 Unrest

During 1919 rioting against black seamen and residents took place in Liverpool (Fig. 43.1), Canning Town, London (Fig. 43.2), Cardiff (Fig. 43.3) and Newport. Homes were destroyed and individuals attacked.

Some soldiers returning from the army felt black people shouldn't have jobs when they themselves were unemployed. There was opposition, too, that some black people had married white people and that their families were living in the cities.

Before the riots ended four people had died as a result. Demands for repatriation were made but, as the newspaper report in Fig. 43.1 shows, only 40 of 200 places reserved in the special ship were taken up.

BLACK AND WHITE AT LIVERPOOL.

POLICE PROTECTION FOR NEGROES

Further trouble between whites and blacks took place in the Upper Stanhope-street district of Liverpool late on Monday night, and yesterday morning two white men and seven negroes were brought up at the police court and were remanded for a week.

Evidence was given to the effect that the district was in an uproar and every coloured man seen was followed by large hostile crowds. In two instances the negroes, on being attacked, pulled out knives and razors and attempted to stab some of the crowd. One was heard to shout, "Come on, you English dogs, I will do for you."

The two white men, WILLIAM KENNEDY and DAVID CLARE, were charged with riotous behaviour. They were in a crowd of about 2,000 persons which assembled outside a coloured men's boarding-house in Jackson-street and commenced to wreck the building. It was alleged that they helped in smashing the windows with stones, and that later, when they gained admission, they helped to break up the furniture. Clare was injured about the head in a fight with the negroes. He was said to have smashed up several chairs and to have struck the inmates with the broken fragments.

Some of the coloured men state that the riots would soon be over if the Government would accede to their request to be repatriated. They are British subjects, they say, and ask for justice and fair play. During the war they obtained employment without difficulty, but with the unemployment which has lately come about there has been bitterness shown towards them, and they are gradually being discharged.

It is stated by a Ministry of Shipping official that a few weeks ago 200 berths were offered at various ports to negroes who wished to return, but only about 40 were filled. Meantime shipowners are being encouraged to employ as many coloured surplus hands on their vessels sailing to the West Indies and Africa as they can possibly accommodate.

The police have issued a warning that severe measures will be taken against anyone attempting to wreck property or to attack members of the coloured community, many of whom are inoffensive and have given distinguished service during the war. Scores of coloured men and women, some of them with their families, have gone to the local police headquarters asking for protection, and last evening over 60 of them were taken into the care of the police.

43.1 From *The Times*, 11 June 1919.

CARDIFF RACE RIOTS.

IRISHMAN AND NEGRO SHOT.

Two deaths have occurred at Cardiff as a result of recrudesence of the racial riots late on Thursday night—one, an Irishman, named John Donovan, and the other an unidentified negro. Donovan was shot through the heart with a revolver bullet fired by a coloured man, and the negro died at King Edward's Hospital yesterday morning from wounds, chiefly in the head.

It was late at night wh— the —ble was —per—

. . .

—— w—us.

Several isolated instances of attacks on coloured men occurred yesterday, and immediately a negro showed himself in the centre of the city he was molested. During the afternoon an open-air meeting of negroes was held. The principal speaker was Mr. RUFUS FERNELL, who said he and many of the coloured men who were being attacked were whiter than some of their whiter assailants. There were some among them who had fought in France, while the deeds of the coloured men who had fought for the British Empire in Mesopotamia and Palestine would never be forgotten. He appealed to the coloured men to obey law and order, and to act as the police told them.

The authorities —

43.2   From *The Times*, 14 June 1919.

43.3   From the *East London Observer*, 16 August 1919.

SERIOUS RIOTING AT CANNING TOWN.

Revolvers, Choppers and Steels at Play.

At the West Ham Police Court on Monday, a riotous scene, in which blacks and whites were concerned, in Canning Town on Saturday afternoon, was described.

It appeared, according to the magistrate, the whole affair arose out of an unprovoked attack on a coloured man, who hit back, and he reminded one of the offenders that the blacks were also subjects of the King, and were entitled to the protection of the law.

Revolvers were fired by blacks, but a police inspector said the weapons were timed over the heads of the crowd.

A dock labourer, Walter James Grantham, of Custom House, was charged with having been drunk and disorderly, and with causing damage at a house of a West Indian, Thomas Pell, in Crown Street.

Pell said he was standing at his door with two other coloured men when Grantham made an insulting remark and passed on. He returned and accused the black man of having laughed at him, and hit him on the chest. Pell hit back, and was pulled into the house by his friends, whereupon Grantham smashed the window, broke a flower stand, picked up a guitar, and broke more glass.

A large and disorderly crowd then assembled, and coloured men were attacked wherever they were found, the police soon finding themselves powerless to check the disorder.

Grantham pleaded guilty to being drunk, and said that the black man hit him and he struck back.

Mr. Ratcliffe Cousins: What did you do during the war?

Prisoner: Stevedoring.

Mr. Ratcliffe Cousins: Making good money while other men were risking their lives. These inhabitants of Jamaica, continued the magistrate, were British subjects and entitled to equal treatment by the law. During the war the coloured races of the Empire had done splendid service, and it was a very shabby thing for those who had loafed about the docks to turn round on them. He (Grantham) would be sent to prison for two months with hard labour.

Grantham's wife, who ran out and hit a black man when someone said, "Come quick; Wally is killed; they are shooting the people," was discharged with a caution.

Three coloured West Indian seamen were charged with discharging revolvers, and it was pleaded that they had been chased by the crowd for a quarter of a mile, and the shots were over the heads of the people.

Mr. Daybell, defending, said a number of butchers with choppers and steels joined with the crowd, and the men felt they were in great peril.

Fining two of the men 20s. for having revolvers without a licence, Mr. Ratcliffe Cousins said he regarded their conduct as the acts of desperate men in danger of violence.

44 Confusion

In the 'twenties unemployment amongst seamen was very high. The Seamen's Union wanted to restrict employment to British seamen. The government introduced a law in 1925 which made it difficult for aliens (non-British) seamen to work on British ships.

Black people were made to register as aliens even though they were British subjects. The authorities were not interested in whether people had some papers to prove they were British. People were not believed.

Individuals were not able to resist registration. The result was they were unable to get work and could face the possibility of deportation.

It was not until 1931 that an organisation was formed which was prepared to expose the situation black people faced. The League of Coloured People (see pages 76–7) campaigned to restore black British seamen's rights (Figs. 44.1 and 44.2). Members of the league visited Cardiff and reported on the situation. Capt. Evans, M.P. was persuaded to raise the case in Parliament. He showed that black British people were being regarded as aliens because they were black.

It was not until 1938 that the National Union of Seamen gave support to those seamen who had been discriminated against, as can be seen from the following extract:

MINUTES OF MEETING OF SECRETARIES OF THE BRISTOL CHANNEL DISTRICT, HELD AT MARITIME HALL, CARDIFF, FRIDAY, 23 SEPT. 1938, commencing 5 p.m.

Chairman : Mr. W. Jones, District Secretary
Present : Messrs. Butcher, Thomas, Lewis, Highfield, Thoumine

The Chairman stated he had called this meeting of Secretaries only, as what he had to discuss concerned them only, theirs being the duty to carry out what was decided upon.

He explained that for some time there had been a lot of discontent among the Arabs and Somalis on account of the Rota System. As they knew, this last year had been a very poor one as far as shipping was concerned, and on account of these men being given Public Assistance in Cardiff, when any of the ships laid up and the men discharged in other ports, they generally found their way to Cardiff. At the present time we had 460 Coloured men signing at the Labour Exchange at Cardiff and only 180 White Firemen.

We have, out of the 460 Coloured, about half that number who are Arabs or Somalis, the remainder being West Indians, West Africans, Indians, Egyptians and Muscats.

There are also a good number who were getting Public Assistance without signing at the Labour Exchange, and these men had complained about the long period of unemployment they were experiencing, and wished the Rota to be abolished, so that they could have free access to employment the same as other members of the Union.

They also complained that they were not allowed to go to other ports to look for employment, and instanced the Larrinaga Company sending men from Liverpool for their steamers, and that these men were not Britishers.

They contend that a good many men on the Rota now are not Somalis or Arabs, but British subjects, having taken out Naturalisation papers, and the majority of the remainder have Colonial cards, proving they are British subjects.

A long discussion followed, each of the members of the Committee present taking part, and it was finally decided that we should keep a strict watch on the Rota, and that if any of the Coloured members cared to go to other ports, providing they registered at that port, and conformed to the system which was in operation, no obstacles would be placed in their way.

The Chairman stated he wanted the Officials to keep strict watch on ships carrying Arabs and Somalis, and should they think irregularities were taking place, they were to get into immediate touch with the Engineer, and have the matter inspected.

The District Secretary and Mr. Butcher would see that the Rota was worked as strictly as possible, with a view to having everything on a straightforward basis.

There being no further business, the meeting closed at 7.15 p.m.

SOURCE: National Union of Seamen papers, Warwick University.

More information

The Keys, magazine of the League of Coloured Peoples, vol. 3, no. 1, 1935.

(b) **Seven** persons who rightly claim British Nationality, and who have been and are to-day classified by the Cardiff Police as Aliens, were in lawful and regular possession of British Passports when they were so classified. These documents are not now with their rightful owners! Some were forcibly with-held by the Cardiff Police when displayed for inspection as a protest against Alien Classification and no receipts were given for them. The other Passports were mailed to the Home Office in London for renewal, and were acknowledged by letters now held by the persons concerned. Correctly considered by these world-travellers as high and fixed proof of Nationality (irrespective of the date of expiration) when supported by continued and honourable residence in the country, their Passports were never lightly treated or released.

(c) **Thirteen** persons who rightly claim British Nationality, and who have been and are to-day classified by the Cardiff Police as Aliens, were in regular and lawful possession of British Mercantile Marine Identification Certificates, at the time of this classification. THESE documents clearly certify the Nationality of each holder as "BRITISH," and are only issued above the signature and office of a responsible servant of His Majesty's Service. Three of these thirteen possess British Certificates, three possess Passports, and two held Passports which were surrendered during the Alien Registration drive among the Coloured Seamen.

(d) **Fifteen** persons who rightly claim British Nationality, and who have been and are to-day classified by the Cardiff Police as Aliens, have honourable records for Military Service for King and Country. One was at the memorable battle of Jutland; one served three years in Mesopotamia; one carried the British colours against the "BOERS"; Two joined in the British West Indies, and served the British Empire in its military conquest of Africa; Eight fought in the Great War; and Two hold good conduct and long service Medals. One held a letter of gratitude and the thanks from H.M. George V for military service during the

(e) **Nineteen** persons who rightly claim British Nationality, and who have been and are to-day classified by the Cardiff Police as Aliens, have lived in Great Britain longer than ten years. Of these nineteen, three have resided in this country thirty years or more; twelve from twenty to twenty-nine years; and four have lived here between ten and twenty years. As these men are seamen, employment records at various seaports in Great Britain reveal the fact of their residence. One of these men is sixty years of age, of which thirty-seven were spent in England. Fifteen of the thirty-five, originally selected, are married, with from one to seven dependents. In a few cases men, unable to secure employment because of an apparent discrimination against coloured British seamen in favour of non-coloured British seamen, have been out of work and on the dole for four years.

Thirty-five persons whose rightful claims to British Nationality have been forcefully disregarded by the Cardiff Police are now in possession of the Seamen's Continuous Certificate of Discharge—wherein either the Nationality is recorded as British or the place of birth clearly appears. Some fifteen hundred are now forced to carry Alien Cards where the Nationality is unintelligently stated as "SEAMAN," and the place of birth is purposely left unanswered.

METHODS OF THE CARDIFF POLICE IN REGISTERING COLOURED SEAMEN AS ALIENS.

The Cardiff Police employed various methods of inducing coloured seamen to register as aliens. These methods when not glaringly illegal, were at least highly questionable, and in most cases violated the Alien Order 1920 and the Special Restriction (Coloured Alien Seamen) Order 1925.

45.1 Dr. Harold Moody, from *The Keys*, the journal of the League of Coloured Peoples.

When Harold Moody (Fig. 45.1) died in 1947 thousands of people paid their respects at his funeral in Camberwell.

Harold Moody had been a highly respected family doctor in Peckham for thirty years. He had come to England from Jamaica in 1908 to be a medical student at King's College Hospital in London. He excelled there and specialised in opthalmics (the study of eyes).

Harold found difficulty in getting living accommodation because he was black. In Jamaica his family had been devout Christians and it was only with the help of members of the London Missionary Society that he obtained accommodation and friendship. He later became President of that Society.

After qualifying as a doctor he was unable to get a hospital job and so become a specialist. However, he established himself as a family doctor in Peckham, South London.

He married a nurse, Olive Tranter, from Henley-on-Thames and they had six children. As well as being a very popular and busy family doctor he still found time to start and run a nation-wide movement of black people in Britain. Dr Moody was determined to see that black people had equal rights and equal opportunities. You can read about this organisation, the League of Coloured Peoples, on pages 76–7.

All his life Dr Moody was a practising Christian. He was a deacon of the Camberwell Green Congregational Church, President of Christian Endeavour, and spent most weekends preaching in towns all over England. His house in Queen's Road, Peckham, became a meeting place for black people in Britain and black visitors to Britain.

His son, Garth, lives in South London and is a Congregational Church minister.

44.1 From *The Keys*, the journal of the League of Coloured Peoples.

More information

David A. Vaughan, *Negro Victory* (Independent Press, London, 1950).

◀ 44.2 From *The Keys*.

46 The Twenties and Thirties

In the 1930s, at the time of depression, few children anywhere enjoyed a proper holiday. The most they could hope for was a day trip to the country or the sea (Fig. 46.1).

Dr. Moody's League of Coloured Peoples made a special effort to see that black children had the chance of a day out. They visited Epsom Downs (Fig. 46.2) or Bournemouth, and each Christmas parties were held in local communities. Many of these children came from north and east London, but Fig. 46.3 shows pupils at The Holly's, Sidcup, Kent.

Adults faced colour discrimination when they tried to look for the few jobs that were available. The League tried to take up their cases. In the early 'thirties, for instance, most hospitals would not employ black nurses. Pressure from the League changed this for a few years, but in 1938 they had to report that eighteen hospitals still refused to train black girls.

The League published its own magazine called *The Keys*. This reported on the difficulties people faced, but it also gave details of leisure activities such as parties and other social gatherings (Fig. 46.4).

46.1 League of Coloured Peoples' coach trip, from *The Keys*.

46.2   Epsom Downs, from *The Keys*.

46.3   A Kent school.

46.4   An International Youth Gathering in Forest Gate, East London, from *The Keys*.

47 The Call Again

Once again during the Second World War people of the empire were prepared to fight and work for victory (Figs. 47.1–47.3, 47.5 and 47.6).

In 1940 Britain needed all the help it could get as the country faced the threat of Nazism. Black people, in common with other islanders, joined the armed forces. Capt. Arundel Moody, son of Dr. Moody, joined the Royal West Kent Regiment and became the first black commissioned officer.

Men and women came to Britain to work as civilians or in the armed forces. They were welcomed by the vast majority of people. A minority carried on discriminating against black people (Fig. 47.4) despite the fact that it was against such ideas that the war was being fought.

47.2 From *The Times*, 2 December 1941.

WAR AID FROM THE COLONIES

"SPLENDID ACHIEVEMENTS"

A luncheon at the West Indian Club, Whitehall Court, yesterday was made the occasion of warm tributes to the many men and women of our African and West Indian Dependencies who are giving generous and spontaneous service in the Empire's war effort. The purpose of the luncheon was to initiate a Colonial Comforts Fund for their benefit.

The following contributions to the fund were announced:—£1,000 from Lord Nuffield: £500 from Elder Dempster Lines, Ltd., the Consolidated African Selection Trust, and the Sierra Leone Selection Trust, and the United Africa Company: and two cut diamonds from the Diamond Trading Company. The address of the hon. secretary, Sir Norman King, is Halton House, Holborn, E.C.1.

Sir Hanns Vischer, chairman of the management committee, who presided, said that the question of colour had no place in their scheme. They were undertaking this work of providing for the special needs of Africans and West Indians as a duty towards fellow-citizens who were taking their full share in the war for the existence of their Empire. Not a penny of the fund would be consumed in overhead charges.

Lord Trenchard, president of the council, testified to the splendid response of the British Colonial peoples of Africa to the call to fight on the side of liberty. It was our duty to make certain that, while they were fighting, their lot should be as easy and comfortable as we could make it.

Lord Moyne, Secretary of State for the Colonies, said he was glad to hear that there would be no colour bar. The African regiments had shown in the East African campaign the highest qualities of courage and disciplined initiative, and had not yet had the full credit they deserved for their splendid achievements.

A great amount of valuable war work was being done by men of African descent in ways less prominent in the public eye. Lord Moyne continued. We had had hundreds of highly skilled technicians from the West Indies and Africa, thousands of seamen who were continually facing the terrible dangers of submarines, hundreds from the West Indies who had come over to join the Royal Air Force.

COLONIAL WAR EFFORT

LORD MOYNE, Secretary of State for t Colonies, said that the Nazi effort to destr the City of Westminster had not interfer with the traditional ceremony with which I Majesty opened Parliament. As befitted o present state of war, to-day's proceedings h been shorn of some of their tradition pageantry, but never could Parliament ha met their Sovereign with a deeper feeling loyalty and patriotism. (Cheers.) We shou never forget the way in which during t year the King and Queen had shared to t full the anxieties and the dangers of th people, and how they had never spared the selves in encouraging the nation in its effo (Cheers.)

The House would have heard with gr interest and appreciation what Lord Fitza had said about religious development Russia. The war effort of both great countr would profit by the closer sympathies wh would inevitably develop in our outlook other problems of life.

People were not always sufficiently inform on what the Colonies and Dependencies h been doing. A great expansion had tak place in our African troops, and tens thousands of men of the African races n supplied man-power not only for the infan but for the technical services as well. Th achievements in Eritrea and Somalila showed their efficiency and gallantry. It v the same story throughout the Empire. Rem Dependencies in the Atlantic and Pacific I raised units according to their resources a needs. Several days each week he welcon at the Colonial Office parties of volunteers many races who had come, often at their o expense, to join the R.A.F. and other fight units. We had also been reinforced hundreds of technicians, timber workers, a other skilled personnel.

The great resources of man-power av. able in the Colonial Empire must be used only for the war effort but in the construc work of peace-time development. He lool forward with confidence to a progress increase in the part played by the Colo peoples. Some of the Colonies could r run their administrations from local resou with little help from outside. Our policy n be so to press on with the improvement educational, cultural, and other facilities t full scope should be given to the Colo peoples to employ their talents and abili in the interests of their own communities the Empire generally. (Hear, hear.) earnest of this he had in the last few mor been able to recruit to the Colonial O staff in London two men of African race. hoped that process would expand continue. (Cheers.)

47.1 From *The Times*, 13 November 1941.

RECRUITS FROM THE WEST INDIES

Two thousand newly arrived R.A.F. recruits from the West Indies are now in training at an Air Force station in Yorkshire. They are part of the first mass intake of men from the West Indies, and are qualifying as flight and motor mechanics, radio experts, cooks, and clerks.

47.3   From *The Times*, 11 July 1944.

More information

West Indies Towards Victory (a Central Office of Information pamphlet), sub-sections on 'War Work Overseas' and 'On Active Service'.

RECORDER ON COLOUR BAR

FINE ON WEST INDIAN REDUCED

A fine of £5 imposed at Liverpool Police Court on GEORGE ALEXANDER McGUIRE ROBERTS, a 31-year-old West Indian, for failing to attend Home Guard duties without reasonable excuse was reduced at Liverpool City Quarter Sessions yesterday by MR. E. G. HEMMERDE, K.C., the Liverpool Recorder, to one farthing. Roberts was also given the costs of the appeal.

Miss Rose Heilbron, defending, said that Roberts, an electrician in a war factory, joined the Home Guard as a volunteer without compulsion or direction. When asked by his C.O. why he had failed to do picket duty Roberts explained that he had been refused admission to a dance hall because of his colour. He had returned to the hall wearing his Home Guard uniform, but had again been refused admission.

Roberts, in evidence, said that he stayed from Home Guard parades because he had been insulted while wearing the uniform. There was no colour bar in the West Indies.

Mr. L. N. Constantine, the West Indian cricketer, who is a Welfare Officer of the Ministry of Labour, said "Thousands of West Indians are serving in every branch of the forces, and the R.A.F. in particular give them the highest credentials."

The RECORDER, giving judgment, said the case raised in an acute form a question they would have to face hereafter. He was much impressed by Mr. Roberts's remark "You can always tell the better class of people in factories because they do not believe in colour bars and other matters of privilege." Mr. Hemmerde said that he did not understand how in the British Empire, with so many coloured people as its citizens, anything in the way of a colour bar could exist or ever be allowed to exist by any Government that was worth the name of Government. People came over here to risk their lives on behalf of what they proudly call the Mother Country, and he considered it impertinence for any country to accept the aid of coloured people from any part of the world and then to say "Our laws do not enable us to deal with you on terms of complete equality."

47.4   From *The Times*, 2 August 1944.

war-work overseas

At work in a machine shop, Alvin Christie is doing a skilled job in one of Britain's war factories. One of many volunteers from Jamaica.

BESIDES JOINING fighting forces overseas, many skilled technicians have volunteered for service in Britain's war factories and shipbuilding yards—lending their skill to forge weapons of war for the Forces of Freedom. From Jamaica, 200 technicians came to serve in munition factories making tanks, guns and aircraft for the fighting men, and 20 volunteers were recruited in the Bahamas. About 200 men from British Honduras are also coming to the factories.

600 experienced loggers, from British Honduras, are working in the big forests of Scotland, felling trees and preparing them for use in the shipyards, and for pit props in the coal mines. Many of these men have been used to felling trees of six or seven feet in diameter, of mahogany and other hard woods, and they find their present job of cutting soft wood trees, of two feet in girth at the most, child's play! Most of the men brought their own special axes and hatchets, in which they take great pride. They live in big camps in the forests and they have made a great contribution to the war effort with their skill in forestry.

Women, too, have volunteered for war-work overseas. About thirty girls from the West Indies have joined the Women's Auxiliary Forces in Britain. Many others have joined the Red Cross and other nursing services, to care for the wounded fighting men or to nurse civilian casualties caused by air raids. Few women, of course, can leave their homes and families for overseas war-work. But the thousands of women who must stay at home are contributing to the Allied war effort just by looking after their homes and bringing up fine, healthy children. Because when this war is over and victory is assured, it will be the young children of to-day who will help in the building of the world of to-morrow.

Constantine Higgins is from Kingston, Jamaica, and is a skilled fitter. Here he is shown in a tank factory, fitting a wheel to a tank.

From his home in sunny, peaceful Jamaica, Arthur Jones went to take his place at a production bench in a factory somewhere in the north of England.

Desmond Parks, from Belize in British Honduras, volunteered to work in the big forests of Scotland.

47.5 From *West Indies Towards Victory*, a Central Office of

On active service

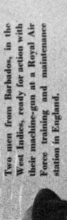

OVER 1,000 MEN and women have volunteered to join the Army and the Royal Air Force in Canada and the United Kingdom. In the Royal Navy and in the Merchant Service are many other volunteers, braving great hazards to carry food and arms to the Allies.

The Colonies have just cause to be proud of their sons and daughters who have been decorated for valour on foreign battlefields. These are some of the decorations that have been awarded to citizens of the West Indies, Bermuda and British Guiana :—

BARBADOS. The Distinguished Service Order to Lieut. J. S. Manning, R.N. (Fleet Air Arm). The Military Cross to Captain J. A. L. Peebles (Dorset Regiment).

BERMUDA. The Distinguished Flying Medal to Sergeant Pilot Watlington (Royal Air Force).

BRITISH GUIANA. The Distinguished Flying Cross to Flight-Lieut. Ian M. MacDougall (Royal Air Force).

JAMAICA. The Distinguished Service Order and the Order of the British Empire to Group Captain J. A. Powell (Royal Air Force).

The Croix de Guerre to Lieut. R. G. Sturdy (Royal Navy).

The Distinguished Flying Cross to Flight-Lieut. Anthony Spooner (Royal Air Force).

The Distinguished Flying Cross to Squadron Leader C. G. S. Rowan Robinson (Royal Air Force).

ST. LUCIA. The Distinguished Flying Cross to Flying Officer Penrith Beauchamp (Royal Air Force).

TRINIDAD. The Distinguished Conduct Medal to Sergeant W. Gilchrist.

Two men from Barbados, in the West Indies, ready for action with their machine-gun at a Royal Air Force training and maintenance station in England.

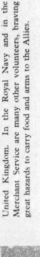

One of the brave merchant seamen from the West Indies learning to fire a Lewis gun, so that he will be able to help protect his ship's valuable cargo from enemy bombers.

Three cheerful Jamaicans who are serving with the Canadian Forces. From left to right, they are Bombardier R. A. Brown, who is a machine-gun instructor, Gunner J. Clarke and Gunner A. Jennings.

The Distinguished Service Order awarded to Lieut. J. S. Manning, R.N. (Fleet Air Arm) and Group Captain J. A. Powell (Royal Air Force).

The Order of the British Empire awarded to Group Captain J. A. Powell (Royal Air Force).

Distinguished Conduct Medal awarded to Sergeant W. Gilchrist.

Distinguished Flying Cross awarded to Flight-Lieut. Anthony Spencer (Royal Air Force).

The Croix de Guerre awarded to Lieut. R. G. Sturdy (Royal Navy).

48 Lord Constantine

Learie Constantine was born at Diego Martin, near Port of Spain, Trinidad, on 21 September 1901.

He travelled to England in 1923 as a member of the West Indies cricket touring team. He returned in the team for the 1928 tour, during which he scored over 1,000 runs and took over 100 wickets.

In 1929 he and his wife, Norma, decided to settle at Nelson, Lancashire. Learie took a job playing cricket in the Lancashire league. He continued to play for the West Indies until 1939, making eighteen Test appearances.

Learie was a member of the League of Coloured Peoples. He took part in many charity cricket matches and was captain of the League's cricket team. Fig. 48.1 shows the West Indian Wanderers cricket team in 1952. Learie Constantine is in the centre of the front row and Theo Campbell (page 84) is on the left of the front row.

48.1   Learie Constantine with the West Indian Wanderers, 1951.

During the Second World War Learie was employed by the Ministry of Labour as a welfare officer for West Indians working in Manchester.

In Figs. 48.2 and 48.3 you can read a report of a 1944 court case in which Learie Constantine was claiming compensation from the owners of the Imperial Hotel, London. As you can see, he had been asked to leave that hotel because he was black. He won his case. Learie was able to demonstrate to the country that racial discrimination was taking place. He was able to use the courts in his fight for civil rights.

48.2   From *The Times*, 22 June 1944.

HIGH COURT OF JUSTICE
KING'S BENCH DIVISION
**WEST INDIAN CRICKETER'S CLAIM
AGAINST A HOTEL**
CONSTANTINE v. IMPERIAL LONDON
HOTELS, LIMITED
Before MR. JUSTICE BIRKETT

HIS LORDSHIP reserved judgment in the action in which Mr. Learie Nicholas Constantine, of Meredith Street, Nelson, Lancashire, claims damages from Imperial London Hotels, Limited, on the ground that the defendants refused to receive and lodge him in the Imperial Hotel, Russell Square, London.

The defendants deny that they refused to receive Mr. Constantine, and plead that, after he had been received in their hotel on July 30 he voluntarily left that evening and was provided with accommodation at the defendants' Bedford Hotel.

Sir Patrick Hastings, K.C., and Miss Rose Heilbron appeared for the plaintiff ; Mr. G. D. Slade, K.C., and Mr. Aiken Watson for the defendants.

Further evidence was given on behalf of the defendants.

Mr. H. Walduck, managing director of Imperial London Hotels, Limited, said that the company also owned the Bedford Hotel, which was almost opposite the Imperial Hotel. He remembered an interview on July 30, 1943, at which Mr. Constantine, Miss O'Sullivan, the manageress, and Mr. Leatherbarrow were present. Mr. Constantine said: " I have a contract for four nights." He (the witness) answered : " There is no question then that you stay for four nights, but incidentally, if you wish to leave to-morrow, I could compel you to pay for four nights." Mr. Constantine stated : " Certainly not, I can leave if I wish." He (the witness) said : " Surely it cuts both ways and I could ask you to leave if I wish." Mr. Constantine replied : " Force would be required before I would leave." He (the witness) felt his own muscle and said : " Well, anyhow, I can't give you a black eye." Mr. Constantine smiled and replied : " No, two negatives make a positive."

Mr. Walduck said that the object of his observation was to relieve the strained atmosphere which had been created. He told Mr. Constantine that the hotel was crowded with 200 or 300 American and Colonial officers and other ranks, and suggested that it might be more congenial to Mr. Constantine to move to the Bedford Hotel which was a comfortable hotel and not so crowded with American officers and other ranks. Mr. Constantine said that wherever he went in the West Indies no restrictions were made on grounds of colour. He (the witness) said that that was not correct as he had stayed at hotels in Jamaica and Trinidad where restrictions were imposed. After a little further conversation Mr. Constantine went to the winter garden for tea.

He (the witness) was sure that Miss O'Sullivan did not use the word " nigger." If she had, it would have struck him as a very offensive term to use. He had not the slightest intention of offering any personal affront to Mr. Constantine. What he desired was to avoid friction and trouble in the hotel.

SIR PATRICK HASTINGS (cross-examining).—Assuming that the evidence given by the plaintiff's witnesses was true, would you agree that Mr. Constantine was grossly insulted in your hotel ?—Yes, if the evidence given was true, but it was not.

The witness said that he never told Mr. Constantine that next day his luggage would be put outside and the door locked against him. That would have been a most offensive thing to say.

After some further evidence Mr. SLADE submitted that the action, being in law an action on the case, was not maintainable without allegation and proof of special damage, which had not been pleaded or proved.

SIR PATRICK HASTINGS said that it was not a correct proposition of law that special damage was an essential element of an action on the case. In some instances the law presumed damage and in others it did not, and the only question was into which class a particular case came. Here it was the plaintiff's right to have access to the defendants' inn, and it was the duty of the defendants to receive him. If the plaintiff's right was denied to him it followed that he had suffered inconvenience for which he was entitled to damages.

His LORDSHIP reserved judgment.

Solicitors.—Mr. Sydney W. Price; Messrs. Durrant Cooper and Hambling.

After the war he became a barrister and continued to expose discrimination. He wrote a book, *The Colour Bar*, in 1954. In 1958 he returned to Trinidad, was elected to Parliament and became Minister of Works and Transport. He came back to England as High Commissioner for Trinidad and Tobago and was knighted in 1962. He resigned the post in 1964 and continued his legal career in Britain. In the late 'sixties he was a member of the Race Relations Board.

He became famous locally and nationally. He was given the freedom of the borough of Nelson in 1963. He was often on the radio, became a governor of the B.B.C. and was made a life peer in 1969.

Learie Constantine died on 1 July 1971.

More information

V. Giuseppi, *A Look at Learie Constantine* (Nelson, 1974).

48.3   From *The Times*, 29 June 1944.

HIGH COURT OF JUSTICE
KING'S BENCH DIVISION

WEST INDIAN CRICKETER'S CLAIM: JUDGMENT AGAINST HOTEL

CONSTANTINE v. IMPERIAL LONDON HOTELS, LIMITED

Before MR. JUSTICE BIRKETT

His LORDSHIP gave judgment for the plaintiff in the action in which Mr. Learie Nicholas Constantine, of Meredith Street, Nelson, Lancashire, claimed damages from Imperial London Hotels, Limited, on the ground that the defendants refused to receive and lodge him in the Imperial Hotel, Russell Square, London, in July, 1943.

It was conceded, for the purpose of the case, that the defendants were innkeepers; that the Imperial Hotel was an inn; that the plaintiff went there on July 30, 1943, and requested the defendants' servants to receive and lodge him; that they had sufficient room for the purpose; and that the plaintiff was ready and willing to pay the proper charges and had paid a deposit of £2. It was further conceded that Mr. Constantine was a man of high character and attainments, a British subject from the West Indies, and that although he was a man of colour no ground existed on which the defendants were entitled to refuse to receive and lodge him.

. . .

His LORDSHIP reviewed the evidence given on both sides regarding what took place at the hotel, and said that he accepted without hesitation the evidence of the plaintiff and his witnesses and rejected that given on behalf of the defendants. He was satisfied that the manageress of the hotel was grossly insulting in her references to Mr. Constantine. It was enough to say that from the outset the manageress made it clear to Mr. Leatherbarrow that Mr. Constantine could not stay in the hotel; that she used the word " nigger " and was very offensive; and that she declined to receive the party and refused to listen to reason. He (his Lordship) also accepted the evidence that Mr. Constantine removed to the Bedford Hotel, on the advice of Mr. Watson and not of his own free will, because of what the manageress and manager said.

In the witness-box Mr. Constantine bore himself with modesty and dignity, dealt with all questions with intelligence and truth, was not concerned to be vindictive or malicious, but was obviously affected by the indignity and humiliation which had been put on him and had occasioned him so much distress and inconvenience, which he most naturally resented.

He (his Lordship) found on the facts that the defendants did refuse to receive and lodge the plaintiff in their hotel without any just cause or excuse, and that Mr. Constantine did not leave voluntarily.

49 Theo Campbell

Theo Campbell was one of the thousands of West Indians who came to Britain to help in the war effort. He was born in Kingston, Jamaica, and volunteered for the Royal Air Force in 1942. The photograph in Fig. 49.1 shows Theo (second from the left) with other members of his graduation class in 1944.

He served in Transport Command, R.A.F. Lyneham, Wiltshire, until 1947. He was then sponsored to attend a business studies course at Balham and Tooting College of Commerce. He was demobbed at Church Lawford, Rugby, in 1948. He did not return to Jamaica, but took a job in the Savings Bank. He was a keen sportsman. He played cricket for R.A.F. Lyneham 1st XI and captained the R.A.F. West Indies team there.

Theo has kept in contact with many people from the Commonwealth. His home in West Kensington was a centre in the early 1950s for former servicemen and students from the Commonwealth. He himself studied economics and philosophy. He moved to Lambeth in 1955. He opened a record shop specialising in blue beat imports and developed a travel agency. His shop became the base for the *West Indian Gazette*, edited by Claudia Jones, and Theo became the sports editor. Since 1966, Theo has edited JOFFA, the magazine of the Jamaica Overseas Families and Friends Association. The stories and information in the magazine range from interviews with such people as Corretta King, widow of Martin Luther King, Lord Constantine, Michael Manley and Lord Pitt, to pictures and stories of community life.

Theo Campbell's family continue to live in Brixton. Theo is active in local politics and community affairs. He takes a particular interest in the Caribbean Ex-Servicemen's Association, the British Caribbean Association and is a governor of several schools.

He was made an Officer of the Order of Distinction by the Jamaican Government in 1975, the first person from Jamaica living overseas to be so honoured.

49.1 Theo Campbell (second from left).

Alfred Moore 50

Alfred Moore.

Alfred Moore was born in Guyana in 1926 and volunteered to join the R.A.F. in 1943 to help fight for Britain. He did his basic training in Trinidad. He then joined a troopship which collected other servicemen from the islands of Jamaica and Barbados. They arrived at Greenock in Scotland later in 1943.

Mr. Moore was sent by train to Melksham in Wiltshire where he completed his basic training. After the passing out parade he was sent to Carew Therrington in Wales. Later he was transferred to R.A.F. Yatesbury in Wiltshire (where he drove a crash tender) and was also stationed at Pembroke and Uxbridge.

At the end of the war he applied to take a commercial art course at the Borough Polytechnic under the R.A.F.'s Educational and Vocational Training Scheme. Although accepted by the college, he was not allowed to take the course because at that time three-year courses were designated as being for officers. Enlisted men were eligible only for six-month courses.

Eventually he was demobbed from the R.A.F. and was accepted on a Government Training Programme to be trained in glass-blowing. During his training he stayed at the West Indian Students' Centre in Wimpole Street, London. Afterwards he worked as a neon signs maker and in the mid 1960s he helped develop perspex fabrication; he is now involved in design and training in this industry.

In 1949 Alfred Moore married Joan Barnes of Hayes, Middlesex, and they have two children. Since 1963 Mr. and Mrs. Moore have been temporary foster parents for the Borough of Kensington and Chelsea and over 200 children have passed through their care. In 1973 they became permanent foster parents.

51 Donald Hinds

Thousands and thousands of black people came to settle in Britain after the Second World War. They came from all over the world. Here is one person's experience from that time.

Donald Hinds was brought up at Richmond Gap, St. Thomas, Jamaica. In his village everyone knew someone who had been abroad. His grandfather had gone to Colon, the American sector of the Panama Canal. Others in the family had gone to Haiti and Costa Rica. He knew that many Jamaicans had gone to Britain to join the armed forces or work in the factories, or to the United States as farm labourers.

Donald went to elementary school. Children could leave school when they were 14. He stayed on until he was 18 as a sort of pupil-teacher. What future was there? He said: 'By the time I left school my mother was already living in London. I did not need much convincing that I'd be better off joining her in London than joining the growing queues for the few jobs there were in Jamaica.' Many Jamaicans were leaving for Britain in the early 1950s.

What was life like in Britain? Donald arrived on the *SS Auriga* at Plymouth in August 1955. He quickly found a job. Brixton Employment Exchange fixed an interview with London Transport. He became the fifth black conductor at Brixton bus garage. It was difficult to get a good place to live. Many white people refused to let houses or rooms to black people. Rents were higher for black people. For entertainment there were many cinemas. The highlight of the week, though, was the Saturday night dance.

Besides the tiring work of being a bus conductor, Donald continued his education. He took O and A levels at Kennington and East London Colleges. He also liked writing for pleasure. In Jamaica he had written poems. In Britain he wrote news articles for the *West Indian Gazette*, *Flamingo*, *Joffa Magazine* and the *Observer*. He contributed to B.B.C. Radio's World Service. He has written many novels and short stories which have not been published.

In 1965 he left London Transport. He wrote a book about the experience of West Indians in Britain. It was called *Journey to an Illusion*. Afterwards he went back to the Labour Exchange for a job. As he was an author, they suggested the Civil Service. Donald then began working in the Post Office Library. He enrolled in the Open University and after three years' part-time study received his B.A. degree. Despite this, promotion in the Post Office did not look too hopeful. Donald trained for teaching and now works in a South London comprehensive school. His wife, Dawn, is also from Jamaica. She has a successful career as a residential social worker. They have a family of three teenage daughters.

51.1   Donald Hinds.

More information

D. Hinds, *Journey to an Illusion* (Heinemann, 1966).

1958 – Violent Threat Again

1958 was the year of racialist attacks in Nottingham and Notting Hill, London. Fig. 52.1 shows how the *Daily Mirror* used history to try to overcome individual prejudice.

DAILY MIRROR, Monday, September 8, 1958 PAGE 13

No. 1: INTRODUCING TO YOU...

THE BOYS FROM JAMAICA

They were born in Jamaica. Do you recognise the uniform?

Smiling Percival Bennett works on a co-operative farm in Jamaica.

● People are human beings even though they come in different colours. The main reason for race riots is plain IGNORANCE of this simple truth.

This is the first of a series which Keith Waterhouse is writing to give people the facts about the coloured people. Today — meet the Jamaicans:

WHEN WAR CAME...

● During the war, 10,000 Jamaicans came voluntarily to this country to fight for Britain.
● Eight thousand of them went into the Armed Forces, and 2,000 into munitions work.

FACTS

● **ARE THEY WASTERS?** In three years, Jamaicans in Britain have sent home £10,000,000 in postal orders to their dependants

● **ARE THEY CRIMINALS?** No Jamaican can leave the island without police clearance. Those with criminal records are not allowed to come.

● **ARE THEY HEATHENS?** Three out of every five Jamaicans are members of a Christian church or group. In Britain, the churches they attend are packed.

● **ARE THEY STEALING OUR WOMEN?** After the war, all the Jamaicans who came here were men. Nowadays, half of them are wives and children—coming to rejoin their husbands.

● **ARE THEY STEALING OUR HOUSES?** Many Jamaicans here live in decrepit houses which white people would not take. Some have done renovations themselves.

● **ARE THEY STEALING OUR JOBS?** Jamaicans today are in steel, coal, Lancashire cotton and public transport. Colour bar or no, there are still few jobs that employers will give to coloured people if they can get white workers instead.

Twenty-two per cent. of the Jamaicans coming to Britain were in white-collar jobs in the West Indies.

But only four per cent. can get office jobs here. Most become transport workers.

And that—according to West Indian welfare workers—accounts for the good manners of Jamaican bus conductors.

FACTS

TOMORROW: Meet the West Africans...

53 Claudia Jones

Millions of people enjoy the carnival at Notting Hill in London every August. It attracts tourists from all over the world. It is the biggest street festival in Europe. Carnival in Britain was started by Claudia Jones and her friends in 1959. Claudia organised five carnivals between 1959 and 1964.

Claudia Jones was born in Trinidad in 1915 and moved to the USA with her family in 1923. When Claudia was twelve her mother died and so she was unable to go to High School. Claudia became a journalist in Harlem, New York City, and worked for a political group called the Young Communist League.

In the USA, during the 1940s, Claudia campaigned for voting rights for African Americans and women's equality; she also spoke out against the lynching of African Americans. During the early 1950s McCarthyism was rife in the USA. This was an anti-communist campaign, led by Senator J. McCarthy. People who were communists or thought to sympathise with communism were persecuted. Many people were dismissed from their jobs or prevented from working. Eleven members of the American Communist Party, including Claudia Jones, were put in prison.

Persecuted alongside Claudia were Robert Oppenheimer, who developed the atomic bomb for the Allies during the Second World War, musician Larry Adler, and film star and singer Paul Robeson. Charlie Chaplin chose to leave America to live in Europe. Claudia did not have a choice. As a British citizen Claudia was deported by the US government to Britain in 1955.

Claudia Jones settled in London. In April 1958 she founded a newspaper for people from the West Indies living in Britain and for all other Black people. It was called the *West Indian Gazette*. It was the first major newspaper for Black people in Britain and sold 15,000 copies a week by 1960. The newspaper was supported by Amy Ashwood Garvey, the widow of Marcus Garvey, Nadia Catouse, Pearl Prescod and Corinne Skinner. Theo Campbell and Donald Hinds contributed to the paper. The *West Indian Gazette* was used to launch the first West Indian Carnival at the Seymour Hall near Marble

53.1 Claudia Jones making a speech in London.

53.2 Claudia Jones (left) with Paul Robeson (singer, actor and filmstar), Amy Ashwood Garvey (first wife of Marcus Garvey) and Ese Robeson in London.

Arch, London, in 1959. The carnival made a direct link to cultural traditions in art, music and dance in the Caribbean. Carnival reflects the history of political ideas about freedom and resistance to slavery. It unified people who were threatened by racial violence in the 1958 riots and horrified by the murder of Kelso Cochrane in 1959.

Claudia continued to campaign ceaselessly for justice and freedom. She tried to prevent racial discrimination in housing, employment and education. She also founded a political group in Britain called the Coloured People's Progressive Association. Claudia campaigned against the imprisonment of Nelson Mandela and tirelessly opposed the 1962 Commonwealth Immigration Act. This last action, involving meetings all over Britain, contributed to her early death. She died at the age of 49 in 1964.

53.3 Claudia Jones (third from left) campaigning at St. Martin-in-the-Fields Church, London. Lord Pitt is directly behind Claudia. The actor Edrich Connor and Pearl Connor are seventh and eighth from the left. Jan Carew, author of *Black Midas* and many other books, is second from the right.

Claudia Jones was buried at London's Highgate Cemetery next to the grave of Karl Marx. Following Claudia's effort in Britain the carnival is now a famous event and there are many Black newspapers, magazines and TV shows.

More information

B. Johnson, *I think of my mother: notes on the life and times of Claudia Jones* (Karia Press, 1985).

J. Tyson, *Claudia Jones 1915–1964: a woman of our times* (Camden Black Sisters Group, 1988).

Books and Resources

A. Alexander and A. Dewjee, *The Wonderful Adventures of Mary Seacole In Many Lands*, Falling Wall Press, 1984.

J. Anim-Aidoo, *Longest Journey: A History of Black Lewisham*, Deptford Forum Publishing, 1995.

J. Ashton Braithwaite, *A Black British Soldier*, 21st Century Books, 1969.

Bradford Heritage Recording Unit, *Destination Bradford*, 1987.

D. Bygott, *Black and British*, Oxford University Press, 1992.

Chapeltown Black Women Writer's Group, *When Our Ship Comes In: Black Women Talk*, Yorkshire Art Circus, 1992.

S. Collicott, *Connections: Haringey's Local, National and World Links*, Haringey Community Information Service, 1986.

D. Dabydeen, *Hogarth's Blacks: Images of Blacks in Eighteenth Century English Art*, Manchester University Press, 1987.

C. Douglas and B. Bousquet, *West Indian Women At War: British Racism in World War Two*, Lawrence and Wishart, 1991.

P. Edwards and J Walvin, *Black Personalities in the Era of the Slave Trade*, Macmillan, 1983.

N. Evans, 'The South Wales Race Riots of 1919', *Journal of the Society for the Study of Welsh Labour History*, Volume 3 No 1, Spring 1980.

M. Ferguson, *A History of Mary Prince: a West Indian Slave Related By Herself*, University of Michigan Press, 1993.

A Ford, *Telling The Truth: The Life and Times of the British Honduran Forestry Unit in Scotland (1941–44)*, Karia Press.

F. Forde (et al), *Black Makers of History: Four Women*, ALBSU, 1987.

P. Fryer, *Staying Power: The History of Black People in Britain*, Pluto Press, 1984.

P. Gilroy, *There Ain't No Black in the Union Jack*, Hutchinson, 1987.

Greater London Council, *A History of the Black Presence in London*, GLC, 1986.

J. Green, 'Some Findings on Britain's Black Working Class: 1900–14', *Immigrants and Minorities*, Volume 9 No 2, July 1990.

J. Gundara and I. Duffield, *Essays on the History of Blacks in Britain from Roman Times to the Mid-Twentieth Century*, Avebury, 1992.

Hammersmith and Fulham Council, *The Motherland Calls: African Caribbean Experiences*, Hammersmith and Fulham Community History Series No. 4 undated.

M. Herbert, *Never Counted Out: The Story of Len Johnson, Manchester's Black Boxing Hero*, Dropped Aitches Press, 1992.

D. Killingray (ed.), *Africans in Britain*, Frank Cass, 1994.

London Borough of Lambeth, *Forty Winters On: Memories of Britain's Post War Caribbean Immigrants*, undated.

G. Lock, *Caribbeans in Wandsworth*, Wandsworth Borough Council, 1992.

D. Lorimer, *Colour, Class and the Victorians*, Leicester Univeristy Press, 1978.

N. Merriman (ed.), *The Peopling of London: Fifteen Thousand Years of Settlement from Overseas*, Museum of London, 1993.

R. McGrady, *Music and Musicians in Early Nineteenth Century Cornwall: The World of Joseph Emidy – slave violinist and composer*, University of Exeter Press, 1991.

North Kensington Archive, *The Caribbean At War: British West Indians in World War Two*, Notting Dale Urban Studies Centre, 1992.

R. Ramdin, *The Making of the Black Working Class in Britain*, Gower, 1987.

M. Sherwood, *Many Struggles: West Indian Workers and Service Personnel in Britain (1939–45)*, Karia Press, 1985.

R. Visram, *Ayahs, Lascars and Princes: The Story of Indians in Britain 1700–1947*, Pluto Press, 1986.

R. Visram, *Indians in Britain*, Batsford, 1987.

R. Visram, *History of the Asian Community in Britain*, Wayland, 1995.

J. A. Western, *Passage To England: Barbadian Londoners Speak of Home*, UCL Press, 1992.

Resource packs, videos, exhibitions and journals

A. Attewell and S. Walker, *Mary Seacole: Teachers' Pack and Learning Resources*, Black Cultural Archives, 378 Coldharbour Lane, SW9 8LF and The Florence Nightingale Museum, 2 Lambeth Palace Road, London SE1 7EW.

Imperial War Museum, *Together: the Contribution made in the Second World War by African, Asian and Caribbean Men and Women*, Imperial War Museum, Lambeth Road, London SE1 6HZ (Multi-media resource pack).

Merseyside Maritime Museum, *Transatlantic Slavery*, Gallery guide, Teacher's Notes, Resources Pack, Merseyside Maritime Museum, Albert Dock, Liverpool L3 4AA.

Nene College, *Moving On: Northamptonshire and the Wider World*, Julia Bush, Nene College, Moulton Park, Northampton NN2 7AL (Book, video and document pack).

Warwickshire Educational Development Service, *Black People in Warwickshire's Past, Part 1*, Manor Hall, Sandy Lane, Leamington Spa, Warwickshire CV32 6RD.

M. Zulfiqar, *Land of Hope and Glory? The Presence of African, Asian and Caribbean Communities in Leeds*, Roots Project, Leeds City Council, 1993.

Caribbean Ex-Servicewomen's Association, *Caribbean Women in World War Two*, Hammersmith and Fulham Council (Video).

Catholic Association for Racial Justice, *Out of the Shadows: An Audio-visual history of the Black Presence in Britain, 1500–1950*, St. Vincent's Community Centre, Talma Road, Brixton, London SW2 (Video).

Royal Albert Memorial Museum, *Olaudah Equiano: Poster and Teacher's Pack*, Royal Albert Memorial Museum, Queen Street, Exeter EX4 3RX.

Merseyside Maritime Museum, *Transatlantic Slavery: Against Human Dignity*, Merseyside Maritime Museum, Albert Dock, Liverpool L3 4AA (Exhibition).

Newsletter, Association for the Study of African, Caribbean and Asian Culture and History in Britain, ICS, 28 Russell Square, London WC1B 5DS (Journal).

Use in education

This book can be used at many levels because it contains a wide variety of images, enlarged text from newspapers and some more difficult handwritten documents.

Pupils and students: You can become a history detective. You can collect on video or tape, or by word processing, the oral histories of people still alive. You can obtain copies of photographs. You can visit your local history library or museum to find out if they have references to unmentioned Black people. You can begin a diary, make up plays or songs that record what happens to Black people or other groups. You can make this into a display for your class or school, for your local library, for the local newspaper or TV station or for the Town Hall, or use it as part of your GCSE coursework for English, social studies or history.

National Curriculum History

Skills: At all Key Stages this book provides a wide range of sources – photographic; reproductions of paintings and prints; reproductions from newspapers, state papers, diaries and contemporary representations – from which pupils can find out about the past (Key Stage 1); ask and answer questions (Key Stage 2); and investigate and evaluate (Key Stage 3).

Key Stage 1: Pupils should be taught about the many famous women and men, drawn from British history, featured in the book. They can use the photographs of the bus, of the school and the prints to make then and now comparisons.

Key Stage 2: Pupils should be taught about social, cultural, religious and ethnic diversity of the societies studied (Key Element 2b):

Life in Tudor Times: Black people as servants and slaves; the role of Hawkins; the Elizabethan Proclamation.

Victorian Britain: Black Victorians: Coleridge-Taylor, Aldridge, Cuffay and Goffe and a case study of both Mary Seacole and Florence Nightingale.

Britain Since 1930: Experiences of black children, women and men in the depression, the Second World War and the 1950s, augmented by oral history; emigration and immigration.

Local history: Experiences of ethnic minorities in Britain.

Key Stage 3: Pupils should be taught to analyse the social, cultural, religious and ethnic diversity of the societies studied (Key Element 2a).

The Making of the United Kingdom 1500–1750: Social change including Black settlement; slavery in Britain; the Elizabethan Proclamation and the Yorke and Talbot Judgement.

Britain 1750–1900: The Somerset Case; the Black Loyalists in the American War of Independence; ethnic diversity and vagrancy; Chartism and William Cuffay; Black personalities in Victorian Britain.

The Twentieth Century World: Black involvement in the two World Wars; Black people during the Depression; Black experiences of Britain since 1945.

Non-European Study Unit – Black Peoples of the Americas: The Black experience in Britain provides complementary and contrasting experiences.

Index